Becoming A Servant

Servanthood and Subservience

James Perry

Becoming A Servant

Copyright © 2018 by James Perry

All rights reserved. No part of this book may be reproduced or transmitted in any form or by any means without written permission of the author.

ISBN 9781732437951

Dedication

Keaton Lucas Barron
(March 21, 2010 – May 11, 2018)

Blessed be the God and Father of our Lord Jesus Christ, the Father of mercies and God of all comfort, who comforts us in all our affliction, so that we may be able to comfort those who are in any affliction, with the comfort with which we ourselves are comforted by God.
Second Corinthians 1:3-4

This book is dedicated to my Great Grandson – Keaton Lucas Barron – Born, March 21, 2010 - Died on May 11, 2018 from incurable Leukemia. He went through countless treatments for 5 ½ years. While the original expectation was that he would be part of the 93% who survived, that wasn't to be.

Even at his young age, his legacy is the kindness he showed and promoted in others. His K-Club page has this summary of Keaton's life:

Throughout his five and a half years of chemotherapy, radiation, t-cell therapy and more, Keaton remained positive, agreeable, hilarious, and sweet. He always put others ahead of himself and fought with grace and courage, never complaining about the countless hospital and clinic visits or missing out on so many life experiences because of his illness. Keaton was a shining example of what it means to live with kindness, courage, compassion, and care for others every single day. Keaton passed away at home on May 11, 2018. He touched many lives, taught others about faith, hope, and never giving up, and leaves a legacy that his family and friends hope to share for years to come.

Keaton Barron in his short life exhibited an acceptance of his adversity and never surrendered his personal commitment to kindness and joy.

Our Grandson – James Lucas (Luke) Barron –after the death of his son - wrote the following letter about and to - Keaton Lucas Barron.

My dear sweet Keaton,

Thank you for showing me what it means to be truly selfless. Your love and compassion for others along with the positivity and joy you lived your life, in the face of everything you had to go through, was absolutely amazing to witness. The cross you had to bear for the majority of your life was, quite simply, unfair. Yet you carried it with such grace and strength, never complaining and continued to move forward. You surpassed anything and everything I could have imagined in a son, and I am eternally grateful that God chose your mother and me to be your parents. I am infinitely proud of you, Keaton. I have loved you since before you were born, and will love you for the rest of my life. Thank you for letting me be your Daddy.

I love you!

Enjoy Heaven, my beautiful boy.

Dad

Table of Contents

Introduction 1
1. Personified Perspective 7
2. Your Will Be Done 11
3. Choosing a Master 17
4. Serving Joyfully 23
5. God's Love 29
6. Intelligent Choices 39
7. A Time to Repent 45
8. A Godly Heritage 53
9. Forgiveness 61
10. Abounding Grace 69
11. Temptation 75
12. Memories 81
13. Nuance and Innuendo 87
14. Practicing Patience 95
15. Decisions 103
16. The Inescapable 111
17. Amazement 117
18. Astonishment 125
19. Powerful Grace 133
20. A Living Legacy 137

21. Loneliness	145
22. Being Alone	155
23. Hearing and Heeding	163
24. Honored	169
25. Perilous Times	175
26. Salt and Light	181
27. Hearers Must Be Doers	189
28. Learning to Pray	197
Epilogue	205

Introduction

Whoever wants to become great among you must be your servant, and whoever wants to be first among you must be your slave, just as the Son of Man did not come to be served, but to serve, and to give his life as a ransom for many.
Matthew 20:26-28

In the social culture, there are many pressures upon one to be successful. It would require one to have life plan as well as having personal contacts that can be advantageous. In politics, the paths to success and significance are paved with the right contacts, the right connections, and the right contributions. This is applicable for other career fields – sports, industry, economy, etc.

This can also be true in the religious culture as one vies for the better and more advantageous position and compensation for ministry. Having the right contacts with wide-spread connections, whether it is the correct approach or not, is an influence that can be of great assistance and benefit to meet one's personal ambitions and goals.

In previous generations, there was a greater emphasis on personal sacrifice. It was a day when "faith missions" was a veiled communication that the person needed prayer and financial support if he or she was to be sustained in their ministry pursuits. Bible Colleges were established and maintained that principle as they encouraged students to emulate the faith principle for life and service. Generations of servants were willing to go anywhere, do any work, at any time and at any personal cost.

The emphasis was placed on the servant having a heart to serve in obedience to God's leading in their lives. It was that conviction that propelled servants such as David Livingston (Africa), William Carey (India) and Hudson Taylor

(China) to set aside personal pursuits and wants to become subservient to the one who had called them to serve Him and who was sending them out to the fields that were ready to be harvested. Was their task easy? Would they encounter hardships and difficulties? Would their resources and health be strained? These were never determining factors in their decision on whether or not they would go to the uttermost part of the world for their Lord and Master, Jesus Christ. Their motivation rested in words captured in a hymn written by Homer W. Grimes:

> *What shall I give Thee, Master?*
> *Thou who didst die for me.*
> *Shall I give less of what I possess,*
> *Or shall I give all to Thee?*

Many servants were willing to give their lives as they set out to do pioneer missionary service. Charles R. Swindoll wrote in a devotional about servanthood (August 2015):

> *Servanthood implies diligence, faithfulness, loyalty, and humility. Servants don't compete, or grandstand, or polish their image, or grab the limelight. They know their job, they admit their limitations, they do what they do quietly and consistently.*

Three illustrations about being a servant are shared in testimonials about the life of John Newton. First is a book written by Grace Irwin (1973), *Servant of Slaves: A Biographical Novel of John Newton*. John Newton (1725-1807), was nurtured by a Christian mother who taught him the Bible. She died of tuberculosis when he was seven years of age. Following her death, he became greatly influenced by his father's image and lifestyle. His father did not subscribe to Biblical values and standards that had been taught by his mother. When John Newton was eleven years of age, he went on the first of six voyages with a merchant navy captain. He had lost his first job in a merchant's office because of his insubordination. It was recorded that his employment was terminated due to his "unsettled behavior and impatience of restraint." This mannerism and pattern would persist for many years in his life. However, it also served him well as a captain of a slave ship. This career would not last very long. He soon sank so low that he became a servant of slaves. It reminds one of the life and proclivities of the prodigal son (Luke 15:11-32).

A second illustration comes from the inscription on John Newton's tombstone that gives a brief summary of his life:

> *John Newton, Clerk, once an infidel and libertine, a servant of slaves in Africa, was, by the rich mercy of our Lord and Savior Jesus Christ, preserved, restored, pardoned, and appointed to preach the faith he had long labored to destroy.*

The third illustration is found in the words of a hymn he wrote, *Amazing Grace*. It serves as a testimonial to the faithful teaching of the Scriptures by his mother and the depth of depravity that his life had reached because of his willfulness and obstinacy. Most hymnals contain five stanzas of the hymn even though he had written at least twelve. Some stanzas not usually sung demonstrate his personal soul-searching:

> *In evil long I took delight*
> *Unawed by shame or fear;*
> *'Til a new object met my sight,*
> *And stopped my wild career.*

> *I saw One hanging on a tree,*
> *In agonies and blood;*
> *Who fixed His languid eyes on me*
> *As near His cross I stood.*

James Perry

Sure, never 'til my latest breath,
Can I forget that look
It seemed to charge me with His death
Though not a word He spoke.

My conscience owned and felt the guilt,
And plunged me in despair;
I saw my sins His blood had shed,
And helped to nail Him there.

One truth we sometimes forget is that most of Scripture was penned amid times of slavery. The Old Testament includes various captivities - Egyptian, Assyrian, Babylonian - and times of bondage that were the reality for God's disobedient people.

The Book of Exodus deals with the slavery known by God's people while they were in Egypt and the harsh bondage they had to endure. The Book of Daniel is about Israel's slavery and captivity by the Babylonians. The prophet Hosea writes about the slavery of God's people. He includes the Lord's direction for him to buy a slave-woman who had been harshly treated and abused by her owners. The New Testament offers guidelines to "masters" about how they should treat their slaves, and how the slaves should respond to their masters (Ephesians 6:5-9). Paul also writes about a runaway slave who had heard the Gospel and responded affirmatively to it. The slave, Onesimus (beneficial, profitable, helpful), was told he must return to his owner and Paul writes a letter to that owner, Philemon (affectionate), to receive him back, not only as a slave but also as a valued brother in Christ.

There is an interesting parallel about slavery to a man and slavery to God - Romans 6:17-22,

Thanks be to God that, though you once were slaves to sin, you wholeheartedly obeyed the form of teaching to

which you were committed. You have been set free from sin and have become slaves to righteousness...For when you were slaves to sin, you were free of obligation to righteousness...But now that you have been set free from sin and have become slaves to God, the fruit you reap leads to holiness, and the outcome is eternal life.

In the following Chapters, there will be discussion about the duties and obligations of the slave/servant of God. Even though one is "free indeed" (John 8:36) in Jesus Christ, obedience to Him is necessary if one is to be a true disciple and a good and faithful servant. To be servant-hearted is not easy but it is required. By the grace of God alone, this can and will be gained. May the Lord enable us to be all of what He wants us to be.

1. Personified Perspective

Then these righteous ones will reply: Lord, when did we ...see you hungry ...thirsty ...a stranger ...naked ...sick... in prison? The King will say: When you did it to one of the least of these my brothers and sisters, you were doing it to me!
Matthew 25:31-46 (NLT)

In Matthew 25, Jesus instructs His disciples on the perspective and role of a servant. He told His disciples that in their service to the broken and marginalized, the hungry, the imprisoned, the sick, and the naked, they will encounter Him. The moment food or care is lovingly offered to a homeless or needy person in Christ's name, the service is rendered to Jesus Himself. The perspective that should be indelibly traced in one's mind and will is that you are doing it unto Jesus Christ Himself. This is a truth we need to grasp if we are to develop a servant's heart. When that happens, it will radically reconfigure the way one views opportunities for ministry of various kinds to all types of needy people.

As the development of this perspective maturates within one, it will impact the way the poor, sick, hungry, thirsty, naked, imprisoned are viewed and approached. Questions that one should ask and consider include: What is my response to the single parent who is pregnant? How do I view a stranded motorist alongside a highway? What about individuals with AIDS (Acquired Immuno-Deficiency Syndrome) – is there reluctance to reach out to such a person or afflicted individuals? This list could be longer but the prevailing point to these and other realities in life comes back to whether or not we view ministry in these areas as being ministry to Jesus Christ Himself. Service in the name of Christ no longer is a duty to be checked off our spiritual task list. It is an opportunity to encounter and minister to our Savior!

When I was receiving treatment for Lymphoma in a Fusion Center, I asked the nurses about the number of patients seen and treated each day for various maladies requiring infusion. I was surprised to hear them indicate it was more than four-hundred every week. Sitting in the waiting room allowed for observing several people and their body language. One could only wonder about their stage of cancer; their fears; their hopelessness and despair. Some people occupied their waiting time watching the television in the room or using a smart phone or I-Pad. Some tried to sleep. Others just sat alone and expressionless. It is a haunting thought about Jesus' words: "one of the least of these my brothers and sisters." It is convicting that so many were passed by and that an opportunity to serve Jesus Christ by ministering to them was missed.

There can be no rationalization about this obligation. It cannot be relegated to "you" instead of "me". I cannot say "they" when Jesus wants to hear me say "I". I cannot point a finger at what somebody or anybody else should be doing in Jesus' name. I need to stand before a mirror and realize that Jesus is addressing His word and conveying that which is on His heart for me, my focus on others and the temporal needs requiring attention. The words in James 2:14-20 (BSB), reminds us that faith and works are synonymous when it comes to observing and responding to physical needs. The force of this truth is in Verse 17, "Faith by itself, if it is not complemented by action, is dead."

It is inexcusable to believe that one can be viewed as a credible Christian in good standing based solely upon regularly participating in and being supportive of church activities. Paul wrote to believers in Philippians 2:5-11 (NKJV), "Let this mind be in you which was also in Christ who...made Himself of no reputation, taking the form of a servant and came in the likeness of men...He humbled Himself and became obedient..." As one commits to being Christ-like in life and practice, there needs to be a readiness to relinquish one's reputation as the process of servanthood takes place in one's life. Humility and obedience will be included in the process. It might even be likened to the metamorphosis process (in an insect or amphibian) of transformation from an immature form to an adult form in two or more distinct stages. A common example is when a caterpillar becomes a butterfly. In order for the change from a caterpillar to a butterfly to take place, the caterpillar begins releasing enzymes that literally digest nearly all of its own body. What's left (inside a cocoon) is mostly just a very nutrient rich soup from which the butterfly will begin to form. The point to comprehend is that the caterpillar's life is totally sacrificed as the transformation into a beautiful butterfly takes place. In a similar way, there must be a transformation occurring within one's life and relationship to Jesus Christ. We are to become completely changed from what we have been into what He wants us to be and how He wants us to be seen. The end result should be that Jesus Christ is evidenced in the way one's life is lived and by the manner in which compassion and merciful acts of caring ensue.

When Jesus Christ called ordinary men to become disciples who He would make into extraordinary servants, a spiritual metamorphosis (transformation) would occur. The description is detailed in Luke 14:25-33. There will have to be a new view of one's family (verse 26). There will have to be a greater level of commitment as one identifies with the cross and all that signifies (verse 27 and Luke 9:23). There will be the requirement to renounce all one has (or aspired to be or gain) so one will be unencumbered when following Jesus (verse 33).

In May 2011, The Christian Post featured a guest column written by Mark Batterson, *Three Ways To Take Up Your Cross*. He wrote:

First, it means self-denial. I've never met anyone who doesn't want to experience self-fulfillment, but the only path to self-fulfillment is self-denial.
Second, taking up your cross will mean pain. Are you willing to suffer temporal pain for eternal gain?
Third, it means death. You have to die to self every day. How? By allowing your circumstances to help you become more like Christ, especially the circumstances you don't like. Anytime you feel the pain of an insult, disappointment, suffering, physical challenge, failure, injustice, or trial, it's an opportunity to die to pride, ego, sin, self.

Ron Hamilton is a brilliant song writer who reflects the heart and will of Jesus Christ. One his songs is a prayer about servanthood:

Make me a servant like you, Dear Lord
Living for others each day.
Humble and meek, Helping the weak,
Loving in all that I say.

Give me, Lord, a servant's heart
Here's my life, take every part.
Give me, Lord, a servant's heart.
Help me draw so close to You
That Your love comes shining through
Give me, Lord, a servant's heart.

Make me a witness like You, dear Lord,
Showing the love of the cross,
Sharing Your Word until all have heard,
Serving whatever the cost.

Can you – will you make this your prayer? Are you willing to serve Him entirely – completely?

2. Your Will Be Done

Our Father in heaven, hallowed be your name. Your kingdom come, your will be done, on earth as it is in heaven...
Matthew 6:9-14

The Sermon on the Mount contains an important guideline about prayer. Jesus Christ wants His disciples and all His followers to be guarded against vain repetitions when praying. He doesn't want anyone to think there is a special formula that will gain results because of the frequent recitation of any prayer. Some religious traditions violate this guideline through their teaching, requirements and accountability. Jesus is instructing that the prayer He expressed was a model for how one is to pray.

The Lord's Prayer begins with one's identity with the Heavenly Father. Personalized, one would pray: "My Father..." There is also the recognition of the place where the Father resides, "In Heaven." It should convey that He alone is higher than any principality or earthly power. It is the confirmation of Paul's writing in Colossians 1:15-20 about the eternity, superiority and preeminence of The Creator who we are privileged to reverently reference as: "My Father."

The first three petitions focus on Who the Father is and that which one should always acknowledge about Him when prayer is being offered. The Heavenly Father should hear from His children words of conviction, commitment, worship and submission expressed as: (a) Worship: Your Name – Hallowed; (b) Anticipation: Your Kingdom – Come; and (c) Submission: Your Will – be done on earth as it is in Your heaven.

The petition in Matthew 6 (The Lord's Prayer) will be internalized by Jesus Christ as the time of His crucifixion arrives. Jesus prays, Luke 22:42 (ESV), "Father, if you are willing, remove this cup from me. Nevertheless, not my will, but yours, be done." Jesus had used this necessity in His discourse on His being the bread of life (John 6). In particular, He emphasizes the Father's will and purpose in the Son (John 6:38-40, ESV),

> *For I have come down from heaven, not to do my own will but the will of him who sent me. And this is the will of him who sent me, that I should lose nothing of all that he has given me but raise it up on the last day. For this is the will of my Father, that everyone who looks on the Son and believes in him should have eternal life, and I will raise him up on the last day.*

We should never think of the will of God and the crucifixion of Jesus Christ in the abstract. Jesus wanted His disciples and followers to find their identity through the Cross. His emphasis is that it represents complete sacrifice. In Romans 12:1-2 (NKJV), Paul emphasizes two necessities to glean the meaning of complete sacrifice:

> *Present your bodies a living sacrifice, holy, acceptable to God, which is your reasonable service of worship.*
> *Be transformed by the renewing of your mind, that you may prove what is that good and acceptable and perfect will of God.*

The crucified life requires a cross and death. This is to be the goal and commitment for every Biblical Christian. Dr. A. W. Tozer wrote, <u>The Crucified Life: How To Live Out A Deeper Christian Experience</u>:

> *If I were to choose my cross and the time of my crucifixion, I would always choose the lesser of two evils. But when the Holy Spirit chooses, He chooses both the time of the crucifixion and the cross upon which He will crucify us. Our responsibility is to yield to His*

> *wisdom and allow Him to do the work without any advice from us…*
> *Those who seek the deeper Christian life and those who want the riches that are in Christ Jesus the Lord seek no place, no wealth, no things, only Christ…*
> *One important point many fail to understand is that the Bible was never meant to replace God; rather, it was meant to lead us into the heart of God. Too many Christians stop with the text and never go on to experience the presence of God…*

The life that is lived seeking God's will and His glory entails one's total commitment, obedience and consistency. We are to deliberately and consciously be committed to living in the presence of God; meet the demands of determining the will of God and to be conformed to the image of Jesus Christ (Romans 8:29; Colossians 1:15-16). Paul gives testimony to what is required regarding the image of Jesus Christ in one's life. He states in Philippians 1:20 (NIV), "I eagerly expect and hope that I will in no way be ashamed but will have sufficient courage so that now as always Christ will be exalted in my body, whether by life or by death." I am captivated by his phrase "sufficient courage" and how it relates to commitment to Jesus Christ. What is the intention of sufficient courage? The NLT renders it: "that I will continue to be bold for Christ." The AMP translates it: "with courage and the utmost freedom of speech." It is alleged that Winston Churchill stated: "Courage is what it takes to stand up and speak…"

Dr. Tozer was adamant in his teaching about the crucified life and hindrances to it. He wrote:
> *One of the great problems dating back to the Early Church was that of the static Christian (one who is slowed in his spiritual progress). This is a problem we need to face today in the Christian Church. The great challenge is how do we get such Christians interested*

in becoming more than the average run-of-the-mill type of believers we see everywhere.

Does it not seem strange that the generation with the most advanced technology and the easiest-to-read Bible translations is the weakest generation of Christians in the history of our country? Church attendance has never been lower, and the Christian influence in our culture never weaker.

Too often, we give God only the tired remnants of our time. If Jesus Christ had given us only the remnant of His time, we would all be on our way to that darkness that knows no morning. Christ gave us not the tattered leftovers of His time; He gave us all the time all He had. But some of us give Him only the leftovers of our money and of our talents and never give our time fully to the Lord Jesus Christ who gave us His all. Because He gave us His all, we have what we have; and He calls us 'as He is, so are we in this world' (First John 4:17).

How does one embrace and achieve the crucified life? How is the will of God determined? What will one look like who is being conformed to the image of Jesus Christ? When looking into a mirror, will the reflection seen be the radiating of Jesus Christ in us and being seen through us? There are many booklets and pamphlets indicating how one can know the deeper spiritual life. Steps are given on how one can become godly and Christ like. While some of the booklets are useful tools, the Holy Scriptures provide one with basic steps that should be taken. Four of the passages – starting points - are: Proverbs 3:5-6; Psalm 1:1-2; Romans 12:1-2; and Colossians 4:12. One needs to trust the Lord implicitly; to walk in the pathway or righteousness; to spiritually sacrifice one's body, soul and spirit to the Lord unconditionally; and to seek the will of God always and unwaveringly.

Becoming A Servant

In one's personal devotion time, it is useful to have a hymnal nearby. Some of the Hymns were written out of deep personal needs and situations. One Hymn, Deeper and Deeper, that lends itself to the pursuit of the will of God and being conformed into His image was written in 1911 by Oswald J. Smith (1889-1985). All of the stanzas should be read devotionally. Some of the words that can be the prayer and goal for one's life are:

Into the will of Jesus,
Deeper and deeper I go,
Praying for grace to follow,
Seeking His way to know;
Bowing in full surrender,
Low at His blessed feet,
Bidding Him take, break me and make,
Till I am molded, complete.

3. Choosing a Master

No one can serve two masters: Either he will hate the one and love the other, or he will be devoted to the one and despise the other...
                              Matthew 6:24

The term, master, has several possible definitions and uses. It is defined as: "a person with the ability or power to use, or control; an owner of a slave; an employer of workers or servants; a person eminently skilled in something (as an occupation, are, science); a person whose teachings others accept or follow." The context of Matthew 6:24 is focused upon one's submission to God, or subservient to mammon (possessions, money, gold). Most translations express it as: "You cannot love God and money." The Sermon on the Mount deals with basic truths for practical Christian living. One of those truths is materialism versus spiritual commitment "Where one has to maintain a balance of connecting to spirituality and keeping a sufficient distance to materialism."

Socially, master is used and applied in various ways. Annually, there is the Master's Tournament that attracts some of the world's best golfers to Augusta, Georgia where they vie for the Green Jacket and recognition that one is the superior golfer of the year. Master is also used when referring to Chess. A superior and highly skilled individual gains the title of being a Chess-Master. It is an indication of their knowing all the moves and counter-moves of the chess pieces. A Chess-Master can usually checkmate a lesser opponent in three to five moves.

The obvious application intended by Jesus Christ deals with one's spiritual life and who controls it. In Joshua 24, the challenge for the people is whether or not they will follow after idols or turn to the Lord and obey Him. It is a choice the people must make. Their immediate future depended upon their choice – idolatry or the Lord. Joshua challenged them of the necessity to make the correct and wise choice. Note Joshua's chiding and challenging of the people: Verse 14, "Now fear the Lord and serve him with all faithfulness. Throw away the gods your ancestors worshiped beyond the Euphrates River and in Egypt and serve the Lord." In terms of idolatry, Joshua indicates they have a choice of which idol or god they can embrace. In Verse 15, Joshua asserts: "But if serving the Lord seems undesirable to you, then choose for yourselves this day whom you will serve, whether the gods your ancestors served beyond the Euphrates, or the gods of the Amorites, in whose land you are living."

As a way of drawing a line in the sand and challenging them to join him, Joshua states the obvious and his own personal choice (Verse 15), "But as for me and my household, we will serve the Lord." In verses 16-18, the people protest and say to Joshua that the Lord will be their primary focus from this point onward. However, Joshua immediately replies, verses 19-21, they are incapable to make that choice and follow through with it. He is indicating that their past involvement in idolatry has become a habit with them. Joshua stated to the people that if they were sincere and meant what they were saying, there was an act they must perform (verse 23), "throw away the foreign gods that are among you and yield your hearts to the Lord, the God of Israel." Joshua makes the alternative distinction clear when he states simply: Make an intelligent and spiritual choice. "As for me and my household, we will serve the Lord" (verse 15).

What idols do you have in your life and religious practice? How greatly do you cling to and embrace them? Are you willing to throw them away so that you can follow the Lord wholeheartedly? Can you let go of earthly things that hinder your spiritual growth and living in the presence of the Lord?

Becoming A Servant

Will the song and prayer of your heart and life be *Nothing Between My Soul and My Savior* (Written by Charles Albert Tindley, 1905)?

Nothing between my soul and my Savior,
Naught of this world's delusive dream;
I have renounced all sinful pleasure;
Jesus is mine, there's nothing between.

Refrain:

Nothing between my soul and my Savior,
So that His blessed face may be seen;
Nothing preventing the least of His favor;
Keep the way clear! Let nothing between.

Several years ago, J. Allan Petersen wrote a Booklet with the title, *Who Runs Your Life?* with a focus on those things that could impact one's mind, emotion and will. The title was changed later to, *Your Reactions Are Showing* with the same emphasis on anger management, one's bitter resentments and responses, attitudes and feelings of malice. The real danger is that these things can control one and become the master of one's life. One causal result would allow one to ignore the specifics of Ephesians 4:30-31 (NKJV),

And do not grieve the Holy Spirit of God, by whom you were sealed for the day of redemption. Let all bitterness, wrath, anger, clamor, and evil speaking be put away from you, with all malice.

The better and more desirable alternative behavior is stipulated in verse 32, "And be kind to one another, tenderhearted, forgiving one another, just as God in Christ forgave you." One's alternative behavior was dramatically stated and illustrated by Jesus Christ in John 13. The Passover Meal was going to be observed. As the disciples arrived, they were surprised when Jesus Christ assumes the role of a servant and began to wash their feet. Amid the protests offered, Jesus asks the thought-provoking question (verse 12): "Do you understand what I have done to you?" Before they attempt to give a coherent response, Jesus supplies them with the only acceptable response (Verses 13-17):

> *You call me Teacher and Lord, and you are right, for so I am. If I then, your Lord and Teacher, have washed your feet, you also ought to wash one another's feet. For I have given you an example, that you also should do just as I have done to you. Truly, truly, I say to you, a servant is not greater than his master, nor is a messenger greater than the one who sent him. If you know these things, blessed are you if you do them.*

The points Jesus emphatically conveys include: (1) you ought to wash one another's feet; (2) I have given you an example – do as I have done to you; (3) a servant is not greater than his master; and (4) you are blessed if you do that which you know to do.

It is important to know Jesus Christ as one's master as well as teacher and Lord. If the master humbled himself and took on the role of a servant, how much more should His followers be compliant! The disciples understood Jesus Christ was their Master. He was instructing them and sharing practical things or tools for them to use in their ministry as His disciples. Did they always remember who He was? No. Did they have moments of despair when they forgot who He was? Yes.

When I wrote and published the book, *Realizing Significance* (2012), the key text used throughout was Mark 4:35-41. The disciples and Jesus are on a vessel when a sudden storm seems to overwhelm them and jeopardize their lives. Some facts the disciples failed to remember was that Jesus Christ was with them and resting in the stern of the ship - He was actually God in their midst. If only they recalled the reassuring words of Psalm 91:2, "I will say of the Lord, He is

Becoming A Servant

my refuge and fortress; my God in whom I can trust." If only they had recalled that the Lord (Psalm 121:4) "neither slumbers or sleeps." How often are we filled with panic rather than peace? How often do we react to the fear of death rather than confidence in the Lord's deliverance? Jesus, even though He was resting and asleep in the stern of the ship, modelled peace in the midst of the storm. When the disciples had done all they could to keep the ship afloat, they decide to come to Jesus. In their life-threatening moment, they forgot about the several other little boats that were following their larger vessel. They too were in a desperate situation and overwhelmed by the ferocity of the storm. As the disciples rush to Jesus, more than likely they did so with frustration, exhaustion and impatience. They blurt out: "Teacher (Master), do you not care that we are perishing?" (Mark 4:38) What an absurd question to ask of Jesus! Of course, He cares. He has been preparing them for the approaching day when He would be crucified to atone for their sins. The Master cares!

In 1874, Mary A. Baker was commissioned to prepare several songs on the subject of the current Sunday-school lessons. One of the themes was "Christ Stilling the Tempest." She penned the words:

Master, the tempest is raging!
The billows are tossing high!
The sky is overshadowed with blackness,
No shelter or help is nigh;
Carest Thou not that we perish?
How canst Thou lie asleep,
When each moment so madly is threatening
A grave in the angry deep?

Refrain
The winds and the waves shall obey Thy will,
Peace, be still!
Whether the wrath of the storm-tossed sea,
Or demons or men, or whatever it be

James Perry

*No waters can swallow the ship where lies
The Master of ocean, and earth, and skies;
They all shall sweetly obey Thy will,
Peace, be still! Peace, be still!*

Who is your Master? What choice have you made – to follow the culture or to follow Jesus Christ alone? Do you think of The Master as someone who is supposed to serve you and always act in your behalf? Or, do you approach The Master with reverence and confidence desiring to serve Him joyfully? Make your choice today. Echo the words of Joshua, "As for me and my household, we will serve the Lord!"

4. Serving Joyfully

Make a joyful noise to the Lord, all the earth. Serve the Lord with gladness; come into His presence with joyful songs...Enter His gates with thanksgiving and His courts with praise; give thanks to Him and bless His name.
Psalm 100 (Selected)

In all areas of life, choices are made every day. Simple decisions, such as: What shall I wear? Where should I go? With whom should I go? How much expendable money do I have available? Should I spend it for some pleasure or save/invest it for my future needs or choices? Will I enter a new day with exuberance, joyfulness and cheerfulness or with grumbling, misery and sadness?

Jesus Christ made the message of joy central to His ministry. In the midst of His preparation of His disciples for His departure from them, He gave an illustration about the need and source of joy (John 15:1-11). His summation and conclusive statement is stated in verse 11: "These things I have spoken to you, that My joy may be in you, and that your joy may be full." There is a distinction that should be made between joy and happiness. Joy is based upon one's relationship to Jesus Christ. It necessitates that one abide in Christ and knowing that relationship to be growing and progressing. The abiding will assure strength, stability and productivity. Happiness is more dependent on events and circumstances. It is influenced by that which is happening in one's life. A happy individual can know some joy but it is temporary. True joy in Jesus Christ is characterized by its permanence in one's life.

Several years ago, Adrian Rogers preached a four-point sermon based upon John 15:11. His points were: (1) The Source of Joy. Jesus referred to it as "My joy" being in you.

(2) The Stability of Joy. It is not a joy that comes and goes. If He is within you always, His joy is also in you. (3) The Sufficiency of Joy. Not only is His joy here to stay, but the joy of the Lord is always more than enough. (4) The Secret of Joy. "Even though this joy is available to us, not every Christian has joy. You can be a Christian and still be miserable. As a matter of fact, the most miserable man on Earth is not an unsaved man but is a saved man out of fellowship with God. David, after he had committed sin, prayed in Psalm 51:12, 'Restore unto me the joy of Thy salvation.' He hadn't lost his salvation, but he had lost the joy of it."

The importance and benefit of joy becoming a greater reality in one's life is indicative of spiritual growth and development. Joy is a fruit of the Holy Spirit (Galatians 5:22-23) that must be present in one's life and radiating from it. The enjoinder attached to the Spirit-controlled life is given in verse 25, "If we live by (the enablement of) the Spirit, let us also keep in step with the Spirit." The Message paraphrase is: "Since this is the kind of life we have chosen, the life of the Spirit, let us make sure that we do not just hold it as an idea in our heads or a sentiment in our hearts, but work out its implications in every detail of our lives."

Over the years, children have learned a chorus that they sing with enthusiasm: "I have the joy, joy, joy, joy (someone will ask), where?" And the chorus continues: "Down in my heart…to stay." Other stanzas have been added to it, such as: "I know the devil doesn't like it but it's down in my heart." The words express a great truth that should be a real part of every Biblical Christian's life. Where do you have the joy? The response should be: Down in my heart to stay!

There may be times when difficulties, adversity and affliction may be a real part of one's experience and life. Even though these are a possibility physically or culturally, they should never have an adverse effect on one's spiritual life, growth and development. In words that almost sound like an oxymoron, Paul wrote in First Thessalonians 1:6 (NIV), "You became imitators of us and of the Lord, for you welcomed the message in the midst of severe suffering with the joy given by the Holy Spirit." The words that seem to be in conflict are "severe suffering" and the "joy given." One must remember the source of joy in one's life is Jesus Christ. James emphasizes this same tension, James 1:2 (NIV), "Consider it pure joy, my brothers and sisters, whenever you face trials of many kinds, because you know that the testing of your faith produces perseverance." The trials are connected to developing perseverance. Joy remains a constant despite all other things that occur. Why? Because Jesus Christ is constantly present as we abide in Him and He abides in us (John 16).

Another passage that contains these contrasting tensions is Hebrews 12:2 (ESV): "Looking unto Jesus… who for the joy that was set before him endured the cross, despising the shame, and is seated at the right hand of the throne of God." Two things are before Jesus, the cross and being seated at the throne of God. Amid that contrast and tension are the words "for the joy that was set before Him." What was that joy set before Him? His willingness and readiness to be the once-for-all sacrifice for sin; the indignity and intense suffering and death on the cross; and the fact that a person of faith can know and embrace, Second Corinthians 5:15 (NIV), "He died for all, that those who live should no longer live for themselves but for him who died for them and was raised again." This was the joy that Jesus had set before Him.

How does one serve the Lord with gladness? How does the joy of the Lord radiate from and through a child of God? In 2017, John Piper led a study on this subject. Some of his observations about serving the Lord with gladness are:

> *There is a kind of service he doesn't like: murmuring service, bored service, and glum service.* Serve the Lord with gladness. *This is biblical! Are we a biblical*

people, or do we just get our truths from our emotions or non-emotions? Psalm 32:11.
Be glad in the Lord, and rejoice, O righteous, and shout for joy, all you upright in heart! Psalm 37:4, Delight yourself in the Lord, and he will give you the desires of your heart.
That's a command, not a suggestion. It's not, If you don't want to delight in me, that's okay. Go ahead with your house or whatever. It's not an option. It's a command. Joy is not an option. It's a command.
Philippians 4:4, Rejoice in the Lord always; again I will say, rejoice.

Having served as a Pastor for more than fifty years, I have often wondered how the lives of people might have been helped and impacted if those who were members and officers were filled with the joy of the Lord. Ministry can be negatively impacted by those who reluctantly "serve" and whose effort is marginalized and negated because they grumble, murmur, complain, gossip, are bored in Church and glum when it comes to interpersonal relationships or conversations.

As he reflected on his own ministry, Oswald J. Smith (1931) was personally impacted by the words of Paul in Acts 20:24 (KJV and NKJV), "...that I might finish my course WITH JOY, and the ministry, which I have received of the Lord Jesus." The World Net Bible: "...that I might finish my race WITH JOY, and the ministry which I have received from the Lord Jesus." It resonated in the mind of Oswald J. Smith and led him to write words to a Hymn that was based on Psalm 100:2, "...come into His presence with joyful songs..." The words he wrote have served as an ongoing inspiration for many Biblical Christians:

There is joy in serving Jesus
As I journey on my way.
Joy that fills my heart with praises

Becoming A Servant

Every hour and every day.

Refrain:
*There is joy in serving Jesus
Joy; that triumphs over pain,
Fills my heart with heaven's music
Till I join the glad refrain.*

*There is joy, joy - Joy in serving Jesus;
Joy that throbs within my heart.
Every moment, every hour,
As I draw upon His power;
There is joy, joy - Joy that never shall depart.*

If one looks to Christ alone, He who modelled what it means to be subservient and joyful will be honored as His followers emulate Him. The writer of Hebrews (12:2-3) reminds and challenges God's people to joyfully serve Jesus Christ as they:

(Keep on) looking to Jesus, the founder and perfecter of our faith, who for THE JOY that was set before him endured the cross, despising the shame, and is seated at the right hand of the throne of God. Consider him who endured from sinners such hostility against himself, so that you may not grow weary or fainthearted.

5. God's Love

If I speak in the tongues of men and of angels, but have not love, I am a noisy gong or a clanging cymbal. And if I have prophetic powers, and understand all mysteries and all knowledge, and if I have all faith, so as to remove mountains, but have not love, I am nothing. If I give away all I have, and if I deliver up my body to be burned, but have not love, I gain nothing.
First Corinthians 13:1-3

Most have some understanding what is meant by God's love. There is a tendency to embellish His love and to make it more inclusive than definitive. There is a need to follow Biblical principles for one's life. A starting point should be Romans 12:9-10 which instructs that one's love must be genuine. It must be operative as God's love in us expresses itself through us by the affection that is shown by us toward brothers and sisters in Christ. The way we can begin to learn and express this love is by following the example of Jesus Christ. This will be evidenced by the consistency of one's subservience in servanthood. John 13 is illustrative of the servanthood Jesus Christ taught and that He expected His disciples to obey as they expressed their love for one another.

In definitive terms of obedience to Jesus Christ, Dr. A. W. Tozer observed: "So let me say boldly that it is not the difficulty of discovering truth but the unwillingness to obey it that makes it so rare among men." The truth that must be observed and obeyed is foundational to servanthood. In John 13:12-17, Jesus shared with His disciples what the role of a servant entails. To be certain they heard what He was saying, He poses a question: "Do you understand what I have done to you?" He is clear with the response He wants them to give: "I have given you an example, that you also should do just as I have done to you." He then determines whether or not they have learned anything from His example and words as He challenges them with: "If you know these things, blessed are you if you do them." The key word is what one will "do" with what has been heard and seen. The basic lesson of servanthood that He desires they learn is stated in His Words, John 13:33-34,

> *A new commandment I give to you, that you love one another: just as I have loved you, you also are to love one another. By this all people will know that you are my disciples, if you have love for one another.*

The rationale Jesus Christ uses with His disciples is based upon how well they know Him. Do they know Him as their Teacher, Lord and Master? Do they know Him and His humility? Do they know that a servant is never to consider himself to be greater than his master?

Part of the grace, truth (John 1:17) and example (John 13) a servant must know is revealed in the demonstration of God's love (Romans 5:8) as He makes provision by the death of His only-begotten Son for one's deliverance from the consequences and penalty of sin. How is the love of God to be embraced in one's life? Some Biblical passages and instruction for all include:

> *John 15:16-17 - You did not choose me, but I chose you and appointed you that you should go and bear fruit and that your fruit should abide, so that whatever you ask the Father in my name, he may give it to you. These things I command you, so that you will love one another.*

The thrust is the individual implementation and practice of agape love. In 1976, John Walvoord, Christian theologian, pastor and President of Dallas Theological Seminary in Dallas,

TX (1952 to 1986) wrote the words to *Love Was When*. His words captured details in the heavenly purpose and the purpose of Jesus Christ. Some of the lyric includes:

> *Love was when God became a man...Love was when Jesus walked in history...Love was God nailed to bleed and die to reach and love one such as I...Love was God dying for my sin...Love was when Jesus rose to walk with me... Lovingly he brought a new life that's free. Love was God, only He would try to reach and love one such as I.*

All Biblical Christians should make time to regularly reflect on and purpose to understand the love of God from His perspective. One can begin with First John 4:7-11,

> *Beloved, let us love one another, because love comes from God. Everyone who loves has been born of God and knows God. Whoever does not love does not know God, because God is love. This is how God's love was revealed among us: God sent His one and only Son into the world, so that we might live through Him. And love consists in this: not that we loved God, but that He loved us and sent His Son as an atoning sacrifice for our sins. Beloved, if God so loved us, we also ought to love one another.*

In pastoral ministry, there are certain observances that serve to focus one on the meaning and application of God's agape (love). In the Biblical Church and with Biblical Christians, one of the regular places of emphasis on agape (love) is the administration of the Sacrament of the Lord's Supper. Normally, First Corinthians 11:23-32 is read prior to one's partaking of the Communion elements. One emphasis is that no one should ever participate in a frivolous manner. It is not a right one can demand – it is a privilege secured by the sacrifice of Jesus Christ in one's behalf. This is a reason for my inclusion of Second Corinthians 5:14-21. I often use other translations and paraphrases to underscore the significance of the text. It is personally meaningful to reflect upon the Amplified Bible - verses 14-15, 21:

> *For the love of Christ controls and compels us, because we have concluded this, that One died for all, therefore all died; and He died for all, so that all those who live would no longer live for themselves, but for Him who died and was raised for their sake.*
>
> *He (God) made Christ who knew no sin to be sin on our behalf, so that in Him we would become the righteousness of God [that is, we would be made acceptable to Him and placed in a right relationship with Him by His gracious lovingkindness].*

God's agape (love) is emphasized when parents bring their infant child/children to dedicate him/her, as well as themselves, to the Lord. It is a solemn and sobering moment as this duty and responsibility is assumed. As they do so, parents take particular vows before the Lord and the congregation of God's people. One vow the parents are asked and take:

> *Do you now unreservedly dedicate your child/children to God, and promise, in humble reliance upon divine grace, that you will endeavor to set before him/her a godly example, that you will pray with and for him/her, that you will teach him/her the doctrines of our holy religion, and that you will strive, by all the means of God's appointment, to bring him/her up in the nurture and admonition of the Lord?*

Similarly, the congregation of God's people are asked to affirm their vow before God on behalf of the parents and child/children. It means that the congregation, individually and corporately, will also endeavor to set before the little ones a godly example. The people of God are asked: "Do you as a congregation undertake the responsibility of assisting the parents in the Christian nurture of their children?"

There is also the example of Holy Matrimony, a Biblical Marriage where vows are to be taken before the Holy God. Preliminary to the marriage vows being asked and answered, there is usually a Marriage Charge stated publicly to the couple:

(Names of couple) I charge you both to remember, that marriage is more than mere fun and games – but your future happiness is to be found in mutual consideration, patience, kindness, confidence, and affection.

(Man), it is your duty to love (Woman) as yourself, provide tender leadership, and protect her from danger. To be the spiritual head of your home as God wants you to be.

(Woman), it is your duty to treat (Man) with respect, to support him, and create a healthy, happy home.

It is the duty of each of you to find the greatest joy in the company of one another; to remember that in both interest and affection, you are to be one and undivided.

In many Wedding Ceremonies, the officiating Pastor will give a brief homily about how the couple's marriage can and will work. A question that is asked is: Is there any guarantee that you will grow stronger together in your marriage relationship? The answer is – Yes! When I officiate at a wedding, I oftentimes reference a work on marriage written (more than fifty years ago) by Joel Neiderhood - *The Holy Triangle*. His thesis is basic and simple. He places the man and the woman on opposite sides of the base of the triangle. He then asked: What is the best and most successful way to find and realize oneness in your marriage relationship? In his presentation, at the apex of the triangle is Jesus Christ. As the man ascends the side of the triangle, and as the woman does likewise, they will come closer to the apex of the triangle – Jesus Christ. As each individual draws closer to Jesus Christ, they will also draw closer to one another. As they do so, they will find unity and oneness in Jesus Christ. He will be the glue that unites them in marriage and will cause them to be productive and fruitful in their ongoing relationship. In Christ alone, they will find themselves complete in Him and enabled to find greater completeness in their marriage.

In a Biblical Christian wedding, First Corinthians 13:4-8 is a necessary component. The passage contains twelve essentials for mutual (agape) love and understanding. One will find that:
1. Love is patient and kind;
2. Love does not envy or boast;
3. Love is not arrogant or rude.
4. Love does not insist on its own way;
5. Love is not irritable or resentful;
6. Love does not rejoice at wrongdoing,
7. Love rejoices with the truth.
8. Love bears all things,
9. Love believes all things,
10. Love hopes all things,
11. Love endures all things.
12. Love never ends.

There is a marked distinction and vast difference between horizontal love and vertical love. Agape (love) requires a constant vertical relationship and maintenance. The whole issue of how much one can love Jesus Christ is detailed in John 21:15-17. What is the issue? It is whether agape (love) is understood and being expressed, or whether it is a lesser or more casual love (filew = a strong friendship). Jesus wants one to respond with agape (love) that is constant and intimate.

A broader consideration pertains to that which Peter ultimately learned from his exchange with Jesus Christ (John 21). An indication of a lesson learned is given in First Peter 1:8, "Though you have not seen Him, you love (agape) Him;

and though you do not see Him now, you believe in Him and (you) rejoice with an inexpressible and glorious joy, now that you are receiving the goal of your faith, the salvation of your souls." Peter has moved and grown beyond the horizontal (less intimate relationship) love relationship. He progressed to a vertical agape (love) wherein he has also discovered his completeness and fullness in Jesus Christ.

Why is all of this important? The average person has a love (agape) obligation in at least three kinds of relationships. First is with one's neighbors. Mark 12:29-31,

> *Jesus replied, this is the most important: hear O Israel, the Lord our God is one Lord, and you shall love the Lord your God with all your heart and with all your soul and with all your mind and with all your strength. The second is this: love (agape) your neighbor as yourself. No other commandment is greater than these.*

A second obligation is to one's enemies. In Matthew 5:43-45, Jesus indicates:

> *You have heard that it was said, love your neighbor and hate your enemy. But I tell you, love (agape) your enemies and pray for those who persecute you, that you may be sons of your Father in heaven.*

The third obligation is to one's wife. In Ephesians 5:25-26, the precise manner in which the husband must honor, respect and love his wife is stated: "Husbands, love (agape) your wives, just as Christ loved (agaped) the church and gave himself up for her to sanctify her…"

All three areas – one's neighbor, one's enemy (perceived or in reality) and one's spouse are to be the objects and recipients of agape (love). It means that the vertical agape (love) one has gained in Jesus Christ is to be expressed in all horizontal relationships without exception. On a human level, this would be impossible to do and accomplish. However, such an example can only be accomplished horizontally as an overflow of the vertical example we are required to emulate, namely, godly behavior.

Ephesians 4:17-32 reminds us of the dimensions of godly behavior. There are at least four steps one must take:

- First, to put off the former way of life and the things once enjoyed.
- Second, to be made new in the attitude of your mind (an obvious representation of true righteousness and holiness.
- Third, eliminate anger from one's life. One must also control his/her desires and urges to take that which belongs to someone else. This could be plagiarism where a person uses someone else's work product as though it was his one's own. It could also be the actual taking of someone else's property (land, home, personal possessions). God expects a person to work, doing something useful with one's own hands. Why? To not be a burden to others and to enable one to have something to share with those in need.
- Fourth, a person's language must become sanctified. The personal commitment and obligation is: "Do not let any unwholesome talk come out of your mouths, but only what is helpful for building others up according to their needs, that it may benefit those who listen."

One's words are to benefit others. We are to express words of comfort, encouragement and edification. One is to build others up rather than being critical and/or tearing others down. Anyone willing to listen should benefit from one's expressed words. There is no room or place for gossip about others or negative innuendos. The goal should be those stated in Hebrews 13:7, "Remember your leaders who spoke the word of God to you. Consider the outcome of their way of life and imitate their faith."

What does all of this mean and entail? One aspect is shared in Hebrews 10:23-25 and the hortatory subjunctives being used. A hortatory subjunctive is a statement urging others to join in some action (commanding oneself and one's associates. It is roughly the same as first person imperative, which does not exist in Greek). Hortatory subjunctives are easily identifiable in Scripture because they usually begin with the brief phrase, "Let us." Hebrews 10 contains these instructions/commands for us:

- *LET US hold resolutely to the hope we confess, for He who promised is faithful.*

This underscores the faithfulness of God for all His people in all situations. He was, is and always will be dependable and faithful. We are to emulate His faithfulness and be an example of it to all others.

- *LET US consider how to spur one another on to love and good deeds.*
- We are to be benevolent and caring people, as well as being generous in our sharing. We are to be known by the consistency of our encouraging others and spurring God's people to participate with you in a care and share ministry.
- *LET US not neglect meeting together, as some have made a habit of doing.*
- There must be regularity and consistency in our presence in God's place of worship. By doing so, we are being a consistent example to all others in this area and practice.
- *LET US encourage one another, and all the more as you see the Day approaching.*
- At the very least, it will be a more intense display of encouraging all the more as the day of the Lord ap-

proaches. Not knowing when that day and hour will be, we need to be diligent in our encouraging others.

Love, faith and action are all linked together. All of the fruit of the Spirit (love, joy, peace, patience, kindness, goodness, faithfulness, gentleness, self-control - Galatians 5:22-23,) is part of the whole of what one is to be and how one is to love all others. There is a Black Gospel Chorus states:

I wanna give my best to you.
I wanna do what you ask me too.
I wanna go where ever you say,
Say the word, and I'll obey.
I wanna live a life that's real;
I wanna serve you Lord for real;
For you deserve all this and more.
So I give you more, more, more...

May this be the response and commitment of each of us. At the root of its effectiveness is our willingness and readiness to implement love (agape) into our thoughts and actions. Horizontally, God's love will be best observed as our vertical love becomes more and more real.

George Mattheson (1842-1906) wrote words that have application for each of us as we desire to love as He loved and to do that which He wants done.

O Love, that wilt not let me go,
I rest my weary soul on Thee.
I give Thee back the life I owe;
That in Thine ocean depths its flow
May richer, fuller be.

6. Intelligent Choices

Ask and it will be given to you; seek and you will find; knock and the door will be opened to you. For everyone who asks receives; he who seeks finds; and to him who knocks, the door will be opened.
Matthew 7:7-8

In one's spiritual life, important choices must be made by the child of God. One of them is in the area of prayer. A foundational principle for prayer is summed up in three key words: Ask, Seek, Knock. In a recent Decision America Newsletter, Franklin Graham included a comment about Matthew 7:7. He included:

In the early 1970s, my mother shared a powerful quote about prayer from a book she was reading, and my father repeated the thought in some of his sermons and writings: 'A mystery and wonder of prayer is that God often waits until someone asks.' I once heard it said that Heaven's storeroom is full of answers for which no one bothered to ask.

A primary intelligent choice is to obey and practice the clear directives given in First Thessalonians 5:16-18 (NLT): "Always be joyful. Never stop praying. Be thankful in all circumstances, for this is God's will for you who belong to Christ Jesus." By extension, this echoes and amplifies the instruction of Jesus Christ that one should consistently follow the practice of asking, seeking and knocking. When it is done, Jesus Christ stated there will be a heavenly response for that which is sought and desired. It may not necessarily be the response we anticipated, hoped for or wanted. At such a time, one needs to be guarded and careful to prevent any doubt or disappointment in one's continuing to ask, seek and knock. God's appointments should never be blurred by one's personal disappointments.

After the ascension of Jesus Christ, the Book of Acts finds the disciples (apostles) devoting quality time to prayer as they sought the Lord's choices for them. Most of the time, the prayers would be offered during times of distress, threat and persecution. There are evidences of powerful responses when they united in prayer. An example of their urgent praying is recorded in Acts 4:29-31 (NIV),

Now, Lord, consider their threats and enable your servants to speak your word with great boldness. Stretch out your hand to heal and perform signs and wonders through the name of your holy servant Jesus. After they prayed, the place where they were meeting was shaken. And they were all filled with the Holy Spirit and spoke the word of God boldly.

Sometimes there can be a Prayer Meeting where a specific person or need is the sole focus of the prayer. The followers of the Lord gather together and are in agreement as they ask the Lord for His immediate intervention. One example is Acts 12. King Herod already had James put to death. When he saw that the people were pleased, he had Peter seized and placed in prison. His purpose was to have Peter put to death. What should the people of God do in a day of ruthlessness and persecution? Is there any reasonable alternative for them? Is there any reasonable alternative for us and the twenty-first century Church? How do we view any opposition to the Biblical Church and those serving faithfully in it? Do we have a sense of the imprisonment and persecution of Biblical Christians in the world? Is our nation oriented toward prayer? What about the church? When was the most recent time you heard of the church collectively being called to unite in days of prayer and fasting about specific needs in the nation and world?

> *Since 1952, a law was passed in the United States Congress formalizing, encouraging and designating a National Day of Prayer for the nation. It remains as a legal day for prayer observance. The original law was amended to indicate that the Day of Prayer is to be observed on the first Thursday of May. It is so designated by the United States Congress, when people are asked to turn to God in prayer and meditation for the nation and the Lord's guidance and blessing.*

Have you participated in days of specific prayer for specific needs? If so, what were your expectations as and when you united with fellow-believers to pray? The believers in Acts 12 had gathered and met to pray. Their prayer was offered intensely, urgently and fervently for Peter concerning his imprisonment and his imminent death. Acts 12:5 indicates that, "Peter was kept in prison, but the church was fervently praying to God for him." Can people pray fervently without having faith or expectation that their prayer will be heard and answered by the Lord? Can prayer be engaged in more as a tradition or ritual rather than a personal and intimate request being made to the Heavenly Father? Is it done so that something religious is taking place. The motive in prayer is as vital as the act of prayer. Why does one pray? To whom or what, is one praying? What are the specific reasons for the urgent and fervent prayers?

What was taking place as the church prayed fervently for Peter? Did they expect God to hear and answer their prayer? There is an adage that indicates: "The proof of the pudding is in the tasting." As the people are fervently praying, an angel enters Peter's prison cell and awakens him. The angel proceeds to lead him out of the prison and city. At first, Peter thinks it is more of a dream or vision. When he comes to his senses, he realizes the Lord has miraculously delivered him from the prison and King Herod. What should Peter do and where should he go? Should he flee and hide?

The next responses recorded in Acts 12 are fascinating. Peter knows where to go. He assumes correctly that people will be gathered in prayer for him. What Peter doesn't know is that the people who are spending quality time in prayer and doing so fervently have made no assumptions regarding their prayer being immediately answered. Acts 12:12-16 records,

Peter went to the house of Mary the mother of John, also called Mark, where many people were gathered together praying. He knocked at the outer gate, and a servant girl named Rhoda came to answer it. When she recognized Peter's voice, she was so overjoyed that she forgot to open the gate, but ran inside and announced, Peter is standing at the gate! You are out of your mind, they told her. But when she kept insisting it was so, they said, It is his angel. But Peter kept on knocking, and when they opened the door, they saw him and were amazed.

The lesson being taught by Jesus Christ about prayer in Matthew 7:7-8 is precise and simple. The principle of ask, seek, knock is illustrated by the fervent prayer being offered at the prayer meeting and Peter standing at the door of the of the home knocking and seeking to gain admission. He would keep on knocking until the door was opened. Recognizing a prayer answered is vital. The timing of a heavenly response cannot be dictated by the one praying. Prayer entails one to keep on asking, keep on seeking, keep on knocking and the heavenly response will come in accordance with the Lord's plan, will and timing for a person or situation. We are to follow the instruction of Jesus Christ to His followers to ask, seek and knock. As that is faithfully and consistently done, He has promised there would be a response.

Ask and it will be given to you; seek and you will find; knock and the door will be opened to you. For everyone who asks receives; he who seeks finds; and to him who knocks, the door will be opened.

Once again, it may not be the response desired or anticipated. What can we expect will take place as and when we pray? What is prayer? The Westminster Shorter Catechism answer is: "Prayer is the offering up of our desires unto God, for things agreeable to His will, in the name of Jesus Christ, with confession of our sins, and thankful acknowledgement of His mercies." What takes place when prayer is offered in the name of Jesus Christ? Romans 8:26-27 responds:

Likewise the Spirit helps us in our weakness. For we do not know what to pray for as we ought, but the Spirit himself intercedes for us with groanings too deep for words. And he who searches hearts knows what the mind of the Spirit is, because the Spirit intercedes for the saints according to the will of God.

Let us be among those who always remember to follow the directives to: "Always be joyful. Never stop praying. Be thankful in all circumstances, for this is God's will for you who belong to Christ Jesus (First Thessalonians 5:16-18, NLT)." Choose this day whom you will serve and pay homage to. Without hesitancy or reluctance, it should be Jesus Christ seated and reigning as the King of your life and you being subservient to Him at all times and in all things. An intelligent choice is expressed in the words written by Albert Simpson Reitz (1879-1976),

Teach me to pray, Lord, teach me to pray;
This is my heart-cry day unto day;
I long to know Thy will and Thy way;
Teach me to pray, Lord, Teach me to pray.

James Perry

Power in prayer, Lord, power in prayer!
Here 'mid earth's sin and sorrow and care,
Men lost and dying, souls in despair;
O give me power, power in prayer!

Living in Thee, Lord, and Thou in me,
Constant abiding, this is my plea;
Grant me Thy power, boundless and free,
Power with men and power with Thee.

7. A Time to Repent

Jesus asked: Do you think those Galileans were worse sinners than all the other people from Galilee? Is that why they suffered? Not at all! And you will perish, too, unless you repent of your sins and turn to God.
Luke 13:2-3

What does it mean for one to repent? One of the responses is: Repentance means to change one's mind and direction in life, from wanting to sin to not wanting to sin. To achieve this result, there must be a change in behavior and attitude about sin. The Westminster Shorter Catechism asks and answers: What is repentance unto life? The reply is: "Repentance unto life is a saving grace, whereby a sinner, out of a true sense of his sin, and apprehension of the mercy of God in Christ, doth, with grief and hatred of his sin, turn from it unto God, with full purpose of, and endeavor after, new obedience."

A well done Desiring God Devotional is titled: *How To Repent* by John Piper. He began with a basic verse from First John 1:9, "If we confess our sins, he is faithful and just to forgive us our sins and to cleanse us from all unrighteousness." John Piper then wrote:

> *This morning I began to pray and felt unworthy to be talking to the Creator of the universe. Nothing changed until I began to get specific about my sins. So I began to call to mind the commands I frequently break. These are the ones that came to mind.*

Matthew 22:37
Love God with all your heart, soul, mind and strength. Not 95%, but 100%.
Matthew 22:39 –

Love your neighbor as you love yourself. Be as eager for things to go well for him as you are for things to go well for you.
Philippians 2:14
Do all things without grumbling. No grumbling - inside or outside.
First Peter 5:7
Cast all your anxieties on him - so you are not being weighed down by them anymore.
Ephesians 4:29
Only say things that give grace to others - especially those closest to you.
Ephesians 5:16
Redeem the time.
Don't fritter away the minutes or dawdle. So much for any pretensions to great holiness! I'm undone. The sins are specific. They've come out of hiding. I look them in the eye. I'm apologizing to Christ for not doing specific things that he commanded. I'm broken, and I'm angry at my sin. I want to kill it...
Colossians 3:5
Put to death what is earthly in you...
Romans 8:13
Put to death the deeds of the body.
I want to live. That's why I'm a killer - of my sin!
In this conflict, I hear the promise
First John 1:9
If we confess our sins, He is faithful and just to forgive us our sins and to cleanse us from all unrighteousness.

John Piper concluded his devotional with this thought: "Peace Rises. Now, prayer feels possible and right and powerful again."

Confessed and forgiven sin is vital for the Christian life. Servanthood requires that a follower of Jesus Christ is to be an example of His righteousness and godliness. Being a godly example and role model for the younger generation is borne out in the significant wording in Exodus 12:21-28. The families have gathered for instruction regarding the Passover. As the instruction is being given, there is also a parental obligation stated:

> *When your children ask you, what does this ceremony mean? You shall tell them: It is the Passover sacrifice to the Lord, who passed over the houses of the Israelites in Egypt and spared our homes when he struck down the Egyptians.*

If/When the children become more inquisitive and inquire about righteousness and godliness, a parent can point to examples of brothers and sisters in Christ who emulate and epitomize righteousness and godliness. If the children within one's sphere of influence would follow your/my example, will it lead them to Jesus Christ and His righteousness? What will they learn about true repentance from observation of our lives? Will they hear us pray and seek forgiveness as we confess our sins of omission and commission? Will they realize what is true contrition and confession as they hear us pray and notice our repentance, as well as observing our humble walk with the Lord?

As the subject of repentance is considered, there are examples in God's Word for us. Nehemiah 1 is a passage that shares the focus and scope of a prayer of repentance. In Nehemiah 1:3, exiles have come to Nehemiah and shared their burden and concern about the state and condition of Jerusalem, They said to him:

> *Those who survived the exile and are back in the province are in great trouble and disgrace. The wall of Jerusalem is broken down, and its gates have been burned with fire.*

Why are they sharing this report with Nehemiah? Why should he be concerned? How would we respond to such a negative report? Nehemiah's response, (1:4-11 NIV), serves as an example for us. His first reaction was: "When I heard these things, I sat down and wept. For some days I mourned and fasted and prayed before the God of heaven." Nehemiah's prayer models contrition and confession as he pleads before the Lord for the people in distress. His prayer begins,

> *"Then I said: Lord, the God of heaven, the great and awesome God, who keeps his covenant of love with those who love him and keep his commandments, let your ear be attentive and your eyes open to hear the prayer your servant is praying before you day and night for your servants, the people of Israel. I confess the sins we Israelites, including myself and my father's family, have committed against you. We have acted very wickedly toward you. We have not obeyed the commands, decrees and laws you gave your servant Moses. Remember the instruction you gave your servant Moses, saying, If you are unfaithful, I will scatter you among the nations, but if you return to me and obey my commands, then even if your exiled people are at the farthest horizon, I will gather them from there and bring them to the place I have chosen as a dwelling for my Name. They are your servants and your people, whom you redeemed by your great strength and your mighty hand. Lord, let your ear be attentive to the prayer of this your servant and to the prayer of your servants who delight in revering your name. Give your servant success today...*

Nehemiah's prayer is one of true repentance. It is also a prayer for the Lord's wisdom and guidance for him and the exiles. Nehemiah, a cupbearer to the King, went to the king and presented the concerns he had for Jerusalem and the exiles. How the King would respond was in the Lord's hands. The King responds kindly, favorably and generously.

Similarly, another prayer of repentance is Daniel 9:1-11 (NIV). Daniel, and many others have been taken captive by Nebuchadnezzar and are in captivity in Babylon. Darius is now King when Daniel is stirred to seek the face of the Lord. Daniel had been reading from the scroll of Jeremiah, God's prophet. As Daniel absorbs and understands the prophecy, we read: "I, Daniel, understood from the Scriptures, according to the word of the Lord given to Jeremiah the prophet, that the desolation of Jerusalem would last seventy years." As he realizes the approach of the seventieth year, he turns to seeking the Lord with a prayer of contrition and confession. His prayer begins:

> So I turned to the Lord God and pleaded with him in prayer and petition, in fasting, and in sackcloth and ashes. I prayed to the Lord my God and confessed: Lord, the great and awesome God, who keeps his covenant of love with those who love him and keep his commandments, we have sinned and done wrong. We have been wicked and have rebelled; we have turned away from your commands and laws. We have not listened to your servants the prophets, who spoke in your name to our kings, our princes and our ancestors, and to all the people of the land. Lord, you are righteous, but this day we are covered with shame, the people of Judah and the inhabitants of Jerusalem and all Israel, both near and far, in all the countries where you have scattered us because of our unfaithfulness to you. We and our kings, our princes and our ancestors are covered with shame, Lord, because we have sinned against you. The Lord our God is merciful and forgiving, even though we have rebelled against him; we have not obeyed the Lord our God or kept the laws he gave us through his servants the prophets. All Israel

has transgressed your law and turned away, refusing to obey you.

The prayers by Nehemiah and Daniel both contain the repentant elements of contrition and confession. If anything positive is to happen in the future of God's people, there has to be an admission of guilt and a turning from all sin. Sin needs to be dealt with as an offense and affront before the Holy God. Do the prayers of Nehemiah and Daniel mean that all of the people are in agreement with the contrition and confession? No! Will they repudiate the sin by which they offended the Lord? Most of them will! Will they turn from all things promoted by the wicked so they can walk uprightly and with integrity? It is unlikely! Will they gain the sense that unless they repent they will perish? Most of them will.

In 1758, Robert Robinson wrote the words to, *Come, Thou Fount of Every Blessing.* Two stanzas contain words that envision contrition and confession. They recognize the need for repentance and returning to a right standing and fellowship with the Living Lord. May these words serve as a prayer of repentance and commitment.

O to grace how great a debtor
Daily I'm constrained to be!
Let Thy goodness, like a fetter,
Bind my wandering heart to Thee.
Prone to wander, Lord, I feel it,
Prone to leave the God I love;
Here's my heart, O take and seal it,
Seal it for Thy courts above.

O that day when freed from sinning,
I shall see Thy lovely face;
Clothed then in blood washed linen
How I'll sing Thy sovereign grace;
Come, my Lord, no longer tarry,

Becoming A Servant

Take my ransomed soul away;
Send thine angels now to carry
Me to realms of endless day.

8. A Godly Heritage

The Lord directs the steps of the godly. He delights in every detail of their lives. Though they stumble, they will never fall, for the Lord holds them by the hand. Once I was young, and now I am old. Yet I have never seen the godly abandoned or their children begging for bread. The godly always give generous loans to others, and their children are a blessing.
Psalm 37:23-26

A godly heritage or legacy is significant. As the health of Billy Graham limited his activity and as he approached death, he left a poignant and definitive statement about his faith, hope and eternity. He said:
Someday you will read or hear that Billy Graham is dead. Don't you believe a word of it. I shall be more alive than I am now. I will just have changed my address. I will have gone into the presence of God.

When he was asked how he would like to be remembered, he replied:
I hope I will be remembered as someone who was faithful - faithful to God, faithful to the Gospel of Jesus Christ and faithful to the calling God gave me not only as an evangelist, but as a husband, father and friend.
I would like to be remembered for being a person of integrity.

The heritage and legacy of John Newton was a testimony of God's grace toward him. When he acknowledged his need for Jesus Christ to be His Savior, he had the sense of God's call for him to be a minister. While he studied for the ministry, Newton worked as a tide surveyor and then for the next 43 years of his life he preached the Gospel in Olney and London. At age 82, he said: "My memory is almost gone, but I remember two things, that I am a great sinner and that Christ is a great Savior." He understood well the grace of a great God toward him and the completely undeserved mercy and favor of God. Following his death, a tombstone was inscribed with these words: "John Newton, Clerk, once an infidel and libertine, a servant of slaves in Africa, was, by the rich mercy of our Lord and Savior Jesus Christ, preserved, restored, pardoned and appointed to preach the faith he had long labored to destroy."

Aging is a reality that seems to arrive much earlier than one anticipates. A truth that cannot be denied is that the older one gets the less capable one becomes physically. However, if looked at life through a correct prism, it is possible to get better with age. Paul indicated this potential and possibility when he wrote and said (Second Corinthians 4:16 ESV): "Even though our outward man is perishing, yet the inward man is being renewed day by day." Physically, one may begin to have limitations and indications of decay. Spiritually, one will be gaining greater strength in the Lord as God's renewal process continues day by day.

Moses may have had this fact in mind when his words in Psalm 90 were being formed. When he wrote these words, he was probably approaching age 70. Obviously, he had no idea about the longevity of his actual life. He had not calculated that his greatest years were ahead rather than behind him. He spent his first forty years in relative ease and luxury as he lived in Pharaoh's household. When he made a choice to defend his true countrymen and killed the Egyptian who was assaulting them, his personal fears caused him to flee and become an exile (or fugitive escaping Pharaoh's reach). A thumbnail sketch of the life of Moses is stated by Stephen in Acts 7:20-30 (NIV)…

Becoming A Servant

At that time Moses was born, and he was no ordinary child. For three months he was cared for by his family. When he was placed outside, Pharaoh's daughter took him and brought him up as her own son. Moses was educated in all the wisdom of the Egyptians and was powerful in speech and action. When Moses was forty years old, he decided to visit his own people, the Israelites. He saw one of them being mistreated by an Egyptian, so he went to his defense and avenged him by killing the Egyptian. Moses thought that his own people would realize that God was using him to rescue them, but they did not. The next day Moses came upon two Israelites who were fighting. He tried to reconcile them by saying, Men, you are brothers; why do you want to hurt each other? But the man who was mistreating the other pushed Moses aside and said: Who made you ruler and judge over us? Are you thinking of killing me as you killed the Egyptian yesterday? When Moses heard this, he fled to Midian, where he settled as a foreigner and had two sons. After forty years had passed, an angel appeared to Moses in the flames of a burning bush in the desert near Mount Sinai.

In a general way, the life of Moses can be understood in three forty-year segments – 40 years in Egypt and the court of Pharaoh; 40 years in Midian working for Jethro as a shepherd; and 40 years leading the children of Israel in the wilderness and bringing them to the threshold of The Promised Land. The words of Psalm 90 may have been the product of his experiences in Midian and the menial tasks he was doing. His relocation from the court of Pharaoh to Midian via an escape route through some barren land had to be traumatic. It is not a surprise that he would chronicle his personal feelings and his sense of the frailty of life. His words in Psalm 90:9-12 (NIV) are descriptive of his thoughts or mood as he pondered his own future. He may have felt betrayed by his countrymen with whom he tried to connect or frustrated by what he thought was a bleak future and confinement in Midian. Moses wrote:

> *All our days pass away under your wrath; we finish our years with a moan. Our days may come to seventy years, or eighty, if our strength endures; yet the best of them are but trouble and sorrow, for they quickly pass, and we fly away. If only we knew the power of your anger! Your wrath is as great as the fear that is your due. Teach us to number our days,*
> *that we may gain a heart of wisdom.*

If only Moses had known God's plan for his life. If only he could've perceived his opportunity to lead God's people out of their bondage in Egypt into becoming a new nation in The Promised Land. Seventy years was not God's planned life-span for Moses, nor was it eighty years. Moses would have the privilege of ministry with God's people long after his anticipated 70 or 80 years. He would have to learn more about God, His plan and purpose, and less about himself and his view of life. Moses saw the days of his life as being tedious and aimless. It reminds one of the words written several centuries later by John Newton:

> *How tedious and tasteless the hours*
> *When Jesus no longer I see!*

Can Moses have a change of heart and mindset about his life and God's purpose for him? Will he find his way back to where he can be most useful for the Lord and His people? The additional words of John Newton include:

> *Content with beholding His face,*
> *My all to His pleasure resigned;*
> *No changes of season or place*

Becoming A Servant

Moses would go on to learn much more about God as he became God's minister and instrument of deliverance. The man who fled from Egypt because of his fear would be led by God back into Egypt with courage and boldness. He would be the one who spoke to Pharaoh the words of God: "Let My people go!" Moses would also be the one to carry God's inscribed laws and deliver them to God's people. Moses was learning more and more each day what it was to walk and serve by faith alone in God alone.

One important truth that must be gleaned about the life of Moses was that his infancy was nurtured by his own Mother, Jochebed, who was taken by Pharaoh's daughter to be his nursemaid (Exodus 2:1-10). She had the unique privilege of training up Moses (and her other children – Miriam, Aaron) in the way they should go, so that when they were old, they will not depart from it (Proverbs 22:6). This unique action epitomizes the reality of children being a heritage from the Lord. In Psalm 127:3-5, Solomon stated:

Children are a heritage from the Lord,
offspring a reward from him.
Like arrows in the hands of a warrior
are children born in one's youth.
Blessed is the man whose quiver is full of them.

Psalm 128:1-4 also speaks of one's children as representing part of God's blessing for the one who fears the Lord and walks in His ways. Solomon wrote:

Blessed are all who fear the Lord,
who walk in obedience to him.
You will eat the fruit of your labor;
blessings and prosperity will be yours.
Your wife will be like a fruitful vine
within your house; your children will be
like olive shoots around your table.
Yes, this will be the blessing

for the man who fears the Lord.

David shared in Psalm 37:23-26, the importance and benefit for the man who is subservient to the Lord. Such a man can know the reality of being richly blessed by the Lord.

The steps of a man are established by the Lord, when he delights in his way; though he fall, he shall not be cast headlong, for the Lord upholds his hand. I have been young, and now am old, yet I have not seen the righteous forsaken or his children begging for bread. He is ever lending generously, and his children become a blessing.

When you leave this world and enter into eternity, How would you like to be remembered? What will your heritage/legacy be? How old does one have to be to leave a heritage/legacy? When Billy Graham died at age 99, he wanted one word engraved on his tombstone: "Evangelist." My Great Grandson, Keaton Lucas Barron died on May 11, 2018 from incurable Leukemia. His legacy is the kindness he showed and promoted in others. His K-Club page has this summary of Keaton's life:

Throughout his five and a half years of chemotherapy, radiation, t-cell therapy and more, Keaton remained positive, agreeable, hilarious, and sweet. He always put others ahead of himself and fought with grace and courage, never complaining about the countless hospital and clinic visits or missing out on so many life experiences because of his illness. Keaton was a shining example of what it means to live with kindness, courage, compassion, and care for others every single day. Keaton passed away at home on May 11, 2018. He touched many lives, taught others about faith, hope, and never giving up, and leaves a legacy that his family and friends hope to share for years to come.

Becoming A Servant

On January 10, 2014, Billy Graham wrote a Blog that contained *10 Guidelines For Christian Living*. Two of them should be common to each of us as we let them become part of our legacy and model what it is to be a wholesome follower of Jesus Christ.

> *Our lives and appearance should commend the Gospel and make it attractive to others. Live above your circumstances. Don't let your circumstances get you down. Learn to live graciously within them, realizing the Lord Himself is with you.*

Billy Graham (who died at age 99) had committed himself to live his life that would be beyond reproach. Keaton Barron in his short life exhibited an acceptance of his adversity and never surrendered his commitment to kindness and joy. May your servanthood, life and legacy have an impact on future generations. May you be remembered as one who served the Lord wholeheartedly and faithfully.

9. Forgiveness

If you forgive other people when they sin against you, your heavenly Father will also forgive you. But if you do not forgive others their sins, your Father will not forgive your sins.
Matthew 6:14-15

The Lord's Prayer (Matthew 6:12 - NIV) contains a petition: "Forgive us our debts as we forgive our debtors." In Luke 11:4, there is a similar petition given. In some versions, the word "trespasses" is used rather than "debts." Whichever translation one uses, sin and grievances are the subject of the petition. The history of this petition finds its basis in Numbers 14:19 (NIV), "In accordance with your great love, forgive the sin (debts, trespasses, grievances) of these people, just as you have pardoned them from the time they left Egypt until now." Paul would also place emphasis upon the importance of having a forgiving spirit. He wrote, Colossians 3:13 (NIV), "Bear with each other and forgive one another if any of you has a grievance against someone. Forgive as the Lord forgave you." The NLT expresses: "Make allowance for each other's faults and forgive anyone who offends you. Remember, the Lord forgave you, so you must forgive others."

While forgiveness is mandated for the Biblical Christian, it is not always easy to do. Innately, there is a tendency to want to retaliate, to never forget, and to hold grudges. A psychology professor espoused his view that one should project the frustration and blame on the person who caused the friction and tension. A minister was heard to say to a colleague in ministry that if he knew the person's father had died as an alcoholic, he could've really shown love to his colleague. At best, there was a discrepancy in his understanding of the Lord's mandate to forgive. How easily Jesus prayed the words in His trial and crucifixion (Luke 23:34): "Father, forgive them for they know not what they do." The plea for forgiveness conveys the: "ceasing to blame or hold resentment against; to grant pardon for an offense and/or offender." Some synonyms for forgive are: "To absolve, excuse, forget."

In 2014, Psychology Today, the subject of forgive and forgiveness was discussed. Some of the article's conclusions are foreign to Biblical understanding. One paragraph of the report states:

By forgiving, you are accepting the reality of what happened and finding a way to live in a state of resolution with it. This can be a gradual process—and it doesn't necessarily have to include the person you are forgiving. Forgiveness isn't something you do for the person who wronged you; it's something you do for you.

Forgiveness requires feeling - being willing to forgive. Sometimes you won't, because the hurt went too deep, or because the person was too abusive, or expressed no regret. Do not attempt to forgive someone before you have identified, fully felt, expressed, and released your anger and pain.

The Psychology Today discussion either ignores or is ignorant of Biblical mandates and actions that need to be taken. If one is angry, what is the minimum action one should take? Answer: Ephesians 4:26-27 NIV, "In your anger do not sin: Do not let the sun go down while you are still angry, and do not give the devil a foothold." Another basic point missed by Psychology Today in addressing the issue of forgiveness has to include the feelings of the Holy Spirit and not just how one personally feels. It seems to be intimating outward expressions of an inner activity. In contemplating this possibility, a word of caution is stated in Ephesians 4:30-32 (NIV). There is clear instructions requiring one to be careful and guarded so that the Holy Spirit is not grieved by one's actions and reactions. In the whole concept of forgiveness, the areas mentioned that must be dealt with and put away are: "…all bitterness, rage and anger, brawling and slander, along with every form of malice." The required and expected alternate behavior is: "Be kind and compassionate to one another, forgiving each other, just as in Christ God forgave you."

Jesus has given the basic approach one should take when offenses and grievances have occurred. He gives His instruction in Matthew 5:23-24. "First go and be reconciled to your brother." In Matthew 18:15-18, there are steps one should take to get matters settled between himself and those with whom there is a grievance or offense. First step: "go and confront him/her privately." If that effort is rejected or unsuccessful, the second step is: "take one or two others along" as witnesses. The third step, if necessary is: "If he/she fails to listen, tell it to the church." Total rejection of all these steps by the offender would result in excommunication from the body of believers.

Some offenses can occur as a result of one's egoism and/or narcissism; treatment of others as subservient; use of nuanced words or innuendos about another person; disregard of another; exclusion of someone as incapable or being undesirable. The list of pettiness can be much longer. One's attitude, as well as words, can be harmful and hurtful of another. There needs to be self-awareness of one's own foibles, as well as sensitivity toward how another person might interpret one's attitude and comments. I remember well when a seminary professor cautioned his students that many times truth is expressed in jest. We need to constantly remember and always implement the words of Paul in Philippians 2:3-5, (NKJV):

Let nothing be done through selfish ambition or conceit, but in lowliness of mind let each esteem others better than himself. Let each of you look out not only for his own interests, but also for the interests of others. Let this mind be in you which was also in Christ Jesus...

(NLT) Don't be selfish; don't try to impress others. Be humble, thinking of others as better than selves. Don't look out only for your own interests, but take an interest in others, too. You must have the same attitude that Christ Jesus had.

Are these the words that govern your attitude and actions with your family, friends, church group? Do you consider yourself as being first rather than one among equals? Is deference (humble submission and respect) part of your spiritual DNA? If/when you look into a mirror, what spiritual reflection do you see? Is it the same as what others observe about you? Does it matter to you how you project yourself and are observed by others? Should it matter to you? If one is spiritually sensitive to the mandates and instructions of Jesus Christ for His followers, it should matter. There is a fine line that separates those who commend the egotist and those who resent narcissistic behavior. Jesus Christ is one who resents those who think of themselves as masters rather than servants. The danger is in the words of Jesus and his response for such behavior, Matthew 7:23 (NLT), "I will reply: I never knew you. Get away from me, you who break God's laws." In Matthew 25:45 (NIV) in the parable where the sheep and goats are being separated, Jesus says to the goats: "Truly I tell you, whatever you did not do for one of the least of these, you did not do for me." The difference between doing those things that inflate self-esteem versus humbly doing that which ministers to and with the least of these, is a vast gulf separating sheep from goats.

Becoming A Servant

What is your objective as a child of God? Who do you want to see receiving the glory for deeds done and words spoken? Where is your spiritual treasure located – in yourself or in Christ and His kingdom? Have you let the sun go down on your anger? How long of a time has that been?

There are times in one's life where there is an opportunity to retaliate or take revenge against a known enemy. Just because there is an opportunity to do so does not mean one should exercise that option and use that advantage to do a perceived enemy harm. I Samuel 24 recorded the opportunity David had to kill King Saul. The king let it be known he would pursue David and kill him. Jealousy, rage and the desire to maintain his royal authority were all factors that motivated the king. The scene is described in verses 3 and 4,

> *Saul came to the sheep pens along the way; a cave was there, and Saul went in to relieve himself. David and his men were far back in the cave. The men said, This is the day the Lord spoke of when he said to you, I will give your enemy into your hands for you to deal with as you wish. Then David crept up unnoticed and cut off a corner of Saul's robe.*

David had his opportunity but he also had a conscience that governed his behavior. He was a man after God's own heart and would not violate his values. Despite the threats of a riled and jealous king, David maintained his tender and forgiving heart. Verses 5 and 6, indicate that…

> *David was conscience-stricken for having cut off a corner of his robe. He said to his men: The Lord forbid that I should do such a thing to my master, the Lord's anointed, or lay my hand on him; for he is the anointed of the Lord.*

On another occasion, David is fleeing from his son Absalom. Absalom was determined to kill his father and usurp the throne so he could become king. It is a sad story of a wild and rebellious son who had no respect for his father or God's anointed king. David is fleeing from his own palace and late at night forded the Brook Kedron with a few of his faithful men and followers. His desire was to hide for a while from his rebellious son. II Samuel 16:5-13 (NIV) records an incident of a man's hatred and opposition.

> *A man from the same clan as Saul's family came out…His name was Shimei son of Gera, and he cursed as he came out. He pelted David and all the king's officials with stones, though all the troops and the special guard were on David's right and left. As he cursed, Shimei said: Get out, get out, you murderer, you scoundrel! The Lord has repaid you for all the blood you shed in the household of Saul, in whose place you have reigned. The Lord has given the kingdom into the hands of your son Absalom.*

What should David do? How will he respond to the disrespect and accusations of his opponent? What will govern his actions and reactions toward Shimei? David received an encouragement to react when "Abishai son of Zeruiah said to the king: Why should this dead dog curse my lord the king? Let me go over and cut off his head." David could've given his tacit approval for that response. However, "The king said: What does this have to do with you, you sons of Zeruiah? If he is cursing because the Lord said to him, curse David, who can ask: Why do you do this?" Verses 11-12 are contrary to one's human instinct, but…

> *David then said to Abishai and all his officials: My son, my own flesh and blood, is trying to kill me. How much more, then, this Benjamite! Leave him alone; let him curse, for the Lord has told him to. It may be that the Lord will look upon my misery and restore to me his covenant blessing instead of his curse today.*

The loyal followers of David complied. "David and his men continued along the road while Shimei was going along the hillside opposite him, cursing as he went and throwing stones at him and showering him with dirt." A valuable lesson had been learned by David and was being learned by his loyal followers. David had a tender heart toward the things of God. He understood servanthood and subservience to the Master, the Lord God. He could forgive the wrong being done to him even though there was opportunity and willingness for his men to pursue and kill the disrespectful opponent. Revenge and retaliation was not part of the character of David.

There is another example where forgiveness, rather than any defensive move, is the preferred behavior. The mob has descended and is ready to capture and abuse Jesus Christ.

John 18:3 (NIV), "Judas came to the garden, guiding a detachment of soldiers and some officials from the chief priests and the Pharisees. They were carrying torches, lanterns and weapons." John 18:10-11 records:

Then Simon Peter, who had a sword, drew it and struck the high priest's servant, cutting off his right ear. (The servant's name was Malchus). Jesus commanded Peter: Put your sword away! Shall I not drink the cup the Father has given me?

The same scene is described differently in Matthew 26:50-53,

Then the men stepped forward, seized Jesus and arrested him. With that, one of Jesus' companions reached for his sword, drew it out and struck the servant of the high priest, cutting off his ear. Put your sword back in its place, Jesus said to him: for all who draw the sword will die by the sword. Do you think I cannot call on my Father, and he will at once put at my disposal more than twelve legions of angels?

How would you have responded in that moment of crisis? Did Peter's response represent a human reaction rather than spiritual discernment? Had he remembered all of the instruction Jesus had given to His disciples that should govern their actions and reactions? The basic behavior for the servant of the Lord is subservience to His plan and will. This is a key element of servanthood. When factoring in God's plan and will for His Son and for us, a hymn written by W. F. Lloyd (1824) should be a truth and commitment that the servant of the Lord must embrace.

My times are in thy hand;
my God, I wish them there;
my life, my friends, my soul, I leave
entirely to thy care.

My times are in thy hand,
whatever they may be;
pleasing or painful, dark or bright,
as best may seem to thee.

My times are in thy hand;
why should I doubt or fear?
My Father's hand will never cause
his child a needless tear.

My times are in thy hand,
Jesus the Crucified;
those hands my cruel sins had pierced
are now my guard and guide.

10. Abounding Grace

We do not lose heart. Even though our outward man is perishing, yet the inward man is being renewed day by day. For our light affliction, which is but for a moment, is working for us a far more exceeding and eternal weight of glory, while we do not look at the things which are seen, but at the things which are not seen. For the things which are seen are temporary, but the things which are not seen are eternal.
Second Corinthians 4:16-18

But may the God of all grace, who called us to His eternal glory by Christ Jesus, after you have suffered a while, perfect, establish, strengthen, and settle you.
First Peter 5:10

Over the years, books and hymns have been written, blogs have been posted, sermons have been delivered on the subject of the grace of God. Grace is defined and understood as the freely given and unmerited favor of Almighty God. It requires acceptance and acknowledgement that all grace is found in God alone and bestowed by Him alone into one's life. It is never based upon the works of man or his self-promotion. There are countless events when grace is exhibited where the response could've innately been one of vengeance or vindictiveness. One example where grace surfaced when personal hurt and sense of loss occurred was at the aftermath of a mass murder where a visitor entered a prayer service and Bible study at the Emanuel African Methodist Episcopal Church in Charleston, South Carolina on June 17, 2015. He was a twenty-four-year old white supremacist, Dylan Storm Roof. He had been welcomed warmly by the congregation. However, he had a different motivation than prayer and bible study for entering the church. During the service led by the Senior Pastor and State Senator, Clemente C. Pinckney, Dylan Roof took out a gun and began randomly shooting. He killed nine people and injured another. The Pastor, Clemente C. Pinckney was one of those killed.

 President Barack Obama was invited to attend and speak at a funeral. As might be expected, he offered his reflections on institutional racism, gun control, and the epidemic of mass shootings and killing in America. He claimed that his remarks were not a political speech but a gospel sermon. This was borne out by his frequent return to the subject of grace. Grace as a gift of God. Grace in the face of loss and pain. Grace in the face of evil and hate. The President spoke of the grace that opened the church doors and invited a stranger in and the grace shown by the families of those who had been killed, despite their unspeakable grief. When these families attended Dylan Roof's court trial, they met him with words of grace and forgiveness.

 It was reported that when the President's remarks had reached a crescendo, he paused – it was a very long pause. Was this a moment for him to regain his composure and recover from an emotional state? What was in his mind and heart during the inordinate long pause? To the surprise (and delight) of many, the President began to sing in a low voice the words of a familiar gospel hymn written by John Newton (1779):

> *Amazing grace how sweet the sound*
> *That saved a wretch like me.*
> *I once was lost, but now am found,*
> *Was blind but now I see.*

 The Apostle Paul was very precise when he addressed the subject of God's amazing grace. Ephesians 2:1-10 (NASB) states a person's condition apart from amazing grace, namely, being dead in trespasses and sins (verse 1). That which makes the distinctive and defining difference is found in two words used by Paul. He emphasized: "God who is rich in mercy" (verse 4) and "by grace you have been saved through faith" (Verse 8). When thinking about the rich mercy of God and His grace, some words from hymns come to mind…

Wonderful Grace of Jesus,
Greater than all my sin.

Marvelous grace of our loving Lord,
Grace that exceeds our sin and our guilt.

I was lost but Jesus found me,
Found the sheep that had gone astray.
Threw His loving arms around me,
Drew me back into His way.

Paul (when his name was Saul) had a personal and memorable experience of the meaningfulness of the grace of God when he was confronted by a vision of Jesus Christ on the road to Damascus (Acts 9:1-9, NASB). A summation of his experience and encounter is given in verses 3 through 5,

Suddenly a light from heaven flashed around him; and he fell to the ground and heard a voice saying to him: Saul, Saul, why are you persecuting Me? And Saul said, Who are you, Lord? He said: I am Jesus who you are persecuting.

This would result in the conversion and transformation of Saul from being a persecutor of the church to a proclaimer of God's grace to the church and to as many others with whom he was given opportunity to share the Gospel. Later on, Paul would share his commitment to the Gospel and his ministry when he gave his testimony and statement of commitment to the elders and believers in Ephesus. He was preparing to leave them. He did not know what was ahead of him in terms of risk and danger. He exclaimed to the brethren (Acts 20:24, NASB), "I consider my life of no value to myself, if only I may finish my course and complete the ministry I have received from the Lord Jesus—the ministry of testifying to the good news of God's grace."

His life, commitment and ministry was focused and based upon "testifying to the good news of God's grace." He had experienced God's mercy and grace in a very dramatic way (Acts 9) and felt compelled to share that same message of faith and hope wherever and whenever he could. He would share this compulsion in Romans 1:14-16 (NASB) when he said: "I am under obligation...I am eager to preach the Gospel...I am not ashamed of the Gospel, for it is the power of God for salvation to everyone who believes..."

On November 22, 2014, John Piper was the guest speaker at the ordination of Kempton Turner in East Saint Louis, IL. He spoke on the theme of Acts 20:24, "to testify to the Gospel of the grace of God." He said:

"...make the grace of God — in all its depth and fullness and power — the foundation, the content, and the aim of your ministry...because all salvation from eternity to eternity, and all your ministry depend on it absolutely.

- *Content because this is your witness woven into every message.*
- *Aim because God has taught us in Ephesians 1:6 that we are chosen and adopted to the praise of the glory of his grace...*

The overarching claim about this meaning of grace that I want to make is this: it refers to the truth that God, and God alone, is the decisive cause at the bottom of our election, our new birth, our justification and our daily life of faith and obedience. And by decisive I mean that no human influence — no human distinctive, no human willing, no human feeling, no human acting, nothing outside God whatsoever — is at root decisive in bring about our election or new birth or justification or daily life of faith and obedience.

The underlying and undergirding of all ministry is to emphasize that salvation and redemption is by grace alone, in Jesus Christ alone, and received by faith alone. It is clearly summarized in Ephesians 1:7, *"In Him we have redemption through His blood, the forgiveness of sins, according to the riches of His grace."*

During the scope of his ministry and care of the churches, Paul had the opportunity of speaking to the Corinthians believers about tithing and offerings (Second Corinthians 8 and 9, ESV). His powerful and conclusive statement is given in 9:8, "God is able to make all grace abound to you, so that having all sufficiency in all things at all times, you may abound in every good work." The thrust is obvious. God's grace will abound to you so that you may abound in every good work. We are to be conduits of God's abounding and amazing grace so that it will touch and impact other lives to seek and abound it in as well.

When John the Baptist was giving a statement about Jesus Christ (John 1, NASB), he made the declaration (verse 17) that as the law was epitomized in the life and work of Moses, grace and truth would be manifested and dramatically realized in the life and ministry of Jesus Christ. Moses had read and amplified that which was inscribed on tablets of stone by the finger of God. Jesus Christ would be the demonstration of God's Love (Romans 5:8) by His being the Lamb of God sacrificed on a cross for one's sins.

Paul wrote to Titus about the centrality of God's grace for life and ministry. Titus 2:11-13 (NASB), "The grace of God has appeared, bringing salvation to all men, instructing us to deny ungodliness and worldly desires and to live sensibly, righteously and godly in the present age…" Paul went on to state, Titus 3:5-7 (NASB),

> But when the kindness of God our Savior and His love for mankind appeared, He saved us, not on the basis of deeds which we have done in righteousness, but according to His mercy, by the washing of regeneration and renewing by the Holy Spirit, whom He poured out upon us richly through Jesus Christ our Savior, so that being justified by His grace we would be made heirs according to the hope of eternal life.

The emphasis of both Paul and all Scripture is the centrality of God's grace. Romans 3:24 (NASB) indicates justification is a gift of God's grace through the redemption that is in Jesus Christ alone. The justification and redemption results in one becoming an heir according to the hope of eternal life. It is always by grace alone in Christ alone.

> *Marvelous, infinite, matchless grace,*
> *Freely bestowed on all who believe!*
> *You that are longing to see His face,*
> *Will you this moment His grace receive?*

Refrain:
> *Grace, grace, God's grace,*
> *Grace that will pardon and cleanse within;*
> *Grace, grace, God's grace,*
> *Grace that is greater than all our sin.*

11. Temptation

Let anyone who thinks that he stands take heed lest he fall. No temptation has overtaken you that is not common to man. God is faithful, and He will not let you be tempted beyond your ability, but with the temptation He will also provide the way of escape, that you may be able to endure it.
First Corinthians 10:12-13

The Bible begins with the "very good" creation of God. After the creation of Adam and Eve, He placed them in a perfect environment. They had just one standard (mandate of God) to precisely obey. They also had daily communion and fellowship with the Creator every day. They knew the special reality of being in the presence of God. There would be a moment of testing for Eve and Adam. Would they be fastidious with their special relationship in a perfect environment? Would they conduct their lives according to God's singular mandate for them? Their response would've been affirmative until the serpent appeared to Eve and raised questions that introduced doubt: What did God really say? What did God really mean? Does God want to prevent you from being equal with Him? The issue for Eve and Adam was their need to take a serious God seriously. They could not allow for doubts to be considered or to gain any traction in their lives. If they did, they would lose their innocence and their intimate relationship with their Creator. They needed to emphatically repudiate the serpent and disallow his influence with them.

There's an interesting concept about temptation and why one is susceptible to it. In a brief statement about King Rehoboam, Second Chronicles 12:10 (ESV), "He did evil, for he did not set his heart to seek the Lord." How sad that the king's principle problem was a failure to seek the Lord and to ask for His guidance and help. King Rehoboam did not do so. Neither did Adam and Eve. How should you and I deal with the tempter and temptations he proposes?

Charles Stanley wrote about temptation and offered guidelines of how one can resist it. He suggests that one should identify areas of weakness in one's life. One must recognize which aspects of one's life are easy targets for Satan's attacks. One must also visualize oneself as doing the right thing. Instead of fantasizing about or giving place for the brief pleasures of sin, one should imagine oneself as pleasing God. One must also faithfully and conscientiously read the Word of God daily. No one is able to defend oneself against the enemy's attacks if one doesn't know the Scriptures. When Jesus Christ was being tempted in the wilderness (Matthew 4:1-11), for each temptation offered by the devil, Jesus had a response from Scripture. This is how God's people should respond when temptations try to infiltrate their spiritual well-being.

If there is confusion about temptation and its source, James clarifies how and when temptation takes place in one's life. He wrote (James 1:13-15):

When tempted, no one should say: God is tempting me. For God cannot be tempted by evil, nor does He tempt anyone. But each one is tempted when by his own evil desires he is lured away and enticed. Then after desire has conceived, it gives birth to sin; and when sin is fully grown, it gives birth to death.

James answers the question: What lures me and entices me to disobey God's standards and values? The answer given by James is: "Each one is tempted by his own evil desires." The passage in the NLT uses a phrase: "Our own desires...entice us and drag us away." In Colossians 3:5, Paul describes those things which drag one away from the Lord: "Consider the members of your earthly body as dead to immorality, impurity, passion, evil desire, and greed, which amounts to idolatry." Personal discipline and spiritual commitment are required for one to deal with members of one's earthly body. It is not an either/or situation. One cannot, should not, think that human effort will prevent a spiritual failure. There are personal disciplines one should have in place. Psalm 1:1-2 indicates the basic disciplines and choices one must make in life. These can be summed up in three statements: Walk not! Stand not! Sit not! in places where sin and evil prevail.

One should not attend or desire to view an R-Rated film. One does not have to enter an establishment that violates moral values and standards of God. One does not have to be in a place that lends itself to the unseemly or where immoral activity prevails. Evil desires are innate in everyone. Those desires must be suppressed and removed from one's life. The Biblical instruction that one should always have in mind includes: Galatians 5:16-18, "Walk by the Spirit, and you will not carry out the desire of the flesh. For the flesh sets its desire against the Spirit…you may not do the things that you please." Other passages that expand on this principle are Ephesians 4:22-24 and Colossians 3:5-10. I Peter 1:14 adds: "As obedient children, do not be conformed to the former lusts which were yours in your ignorance."

We so easily forget an oft repeated prayer that is regularly quoted (Matthew 6:13), "And lead us not into temptation, but deliver us from the evil." This prayer has to be more than words that are recited. It must be incorporated into a personal discipline and action. The petition is an appeal for divine strength and enablement to avoid the places of evil and those who champion them. I have often thought and meditated upon the words of David in his personal commitment, reflection and prayer (Psalm 19:12-13),

Who can discern his errors? Declare me innocent from hidden faults. Keep back your servant also from presumptuous sins; let them not have dominion over me!

Then I shall be blameless, and innocent of great transgression.

Not only was this an appeal for personal deliverance from evil and temptation, the context of the Psalm also focused on the law and standards of God that enlighten one's heart, soul and mind. There were times when David would forget or ignore these values and his prayer. They would lead to a crushing spiritual period in his life. Psalm 32 indicates the weight of God's hand upon him for the evil he had done and the way he attempted its cover up. It would be a long journey for him until he finally came before the Lord in his brokenness (Psalm 51) and in need of an outpouring of God's grace. He would acknowledge his guilt of the sins committed and plead for God's mercy and restoration. His heart-cry for God's mercy and grace is expressed in his words, Psalm 51:9-12,

Blot out all my iniquities. Create in me a clean heart, O God, and renew a right spirit within me. Cast me not away from your presence, and take not your Holy Spirit from me. Restore to me the joy of your salvation, and uphold me with a willing spirit.

IF ONLY the followers of Christ would become sensitive to evil desires and rid themselves of them.

IF ONLY one had a heart-cry for God's inner spiritual revival and restoration that would enable one to walk by the enablement of the Spirit and live by faith alone in Christ alone.

IF ONLY there was a renewal in one's seeking after the greater presence of God in one's life.

IF ONLY the Church would literally take a serious God seriously.

IF ONLY the Church became a beacon of light for those who have sunk into the depths of darkness.

Becoming A Servant

IF ONLY the traits of the spiritual life were more obviously observed in the life of the professing Christian.

IF ONLY the people of God would faithfully and wholeheartedly follow Jesus Christ so he would make them that which He wants them to be.

IF ONLY the tired, burdened, weary, downcast would heed the invitation of Jesus Christ (Matthew 11:28-30) and come to Him, learn from Him, take His yoke that is easy and whose burden is light – and follow Him.

IF ONLY the follower and believer would mean the prayer – "Lead us not into but away from temptation." – so that meaning and purpose would return to one's heart soul and mind.

IF ONLY we could sing and believe…
Yield not to temptation, for yielding is sin;
Each victory will help you some other to win;
Fight manfully onward, dark passions subdue,
Look ever to Jesus, He'll carry you through.

Shun evil companions, bad language disdain,
God's Name hold in reverence, nor take it in vain;
Be thoughtful and earnest, kindhearted and true,
Look ever to Jesus, He'll carry you through.

Refrain:
Ask the Savior to help you,
Comfort, strengthen and keep you;
He is willing to aid you,
He will carry you through.

12. Memories

I thank God, whom I serve with a clear conscience the way my forefathers did, as I constantly remember you in my prayers night and day, longing to see you, even as I recall your tears, so that I may be filled with joy. For I am mindful of the sincere faith within you, which first dwelt in your grandmother Lois and your mother Eunice, and I am sure that it is in you as well. For this reason I remind you to kindle afresh the gift of God which is in you through the laying on of my hands. For God has not given us a spirit of timidity, but of power and love and discipline.
Second Timothy 1:3-7

Memories are a real and vital part of who we are. They remind us of our roots, background, family, education and experiences. These are influences that have shaped us into who we are and, to a degree, how we relate to others and function in society and culture. One's life is filled and impacted by all sorts of negative and positive secular thinking, as well as family, societal and cultural influences. How can one arrive at sound and valid judgments as and when crises come their way?

Cultural values have undergone a major change and shift. Bible reading and prayer have been removed from our public schools so that when a mass shooting or some other crises occur, rather than consult with God in prayer and through His Word, we resort to counsellors, sociologists and psychologists who offer resolve from their background and orientation. They seldom, if ever, use a Biblical resolve or perspective. They are true to their professional philosophy. Because of that orientation, there is an absence of anything that can address the spiritual need or vacuum of those who may feel stressed or conflicted.

Crisis management in the United States Military attempts to bridge the gap between the secular and the spiritual. Military psychologists have observed that therapy sessions deal with a diversity of backgrounds which requires consideration of disparate spiritual beliefs and religious orientations. These beliefs and orientations are valuable resources as coping skills are addressed. Psychologists collaborate with the chaplains/clergy as they address the whole person. There is a recognition and acceptance that a person is comprised of more than just mind, emotion and will but also of body, soul and spirit. It would be of great value if the secular world would embrace this complexity of the individual. Jesus addressed it when he stated in Mark 12:30, that one must interact spiritually with all of one's heart, soul, strength and mind. If this concept is absent from the counselor's beliefs and orientation, the end result will be a chasm, void and vacuum that cannot and will not be bridged with secular approaches and conclusions. Many times the diagnosis reached is that a person is dysfunctional and must be treated with some medication that will enable one to cope. Many times it is prescribing Prozac or Ritalin or a combination of the two to fill the void.

A difference that emerges between the psychologists and sociologists is in the defining of dysfunction. What is it? How should it be addressed? Is there a possible remedy? If so, what is it? Sociologists have defined dysfunction in a variety of ways. One possibility offered by them is a conflict theory wherein groups compete for scarce and limited resources, power, and authority. Competition, they believe and conclude, creates inequality and exploitation. Their thinking is that through conflicts and acceptance of the results come benefits. Even if conflict resolution is not the primary focus, there are other factors sociologists promote. One is dysfunction or the harmful consequences of people's actions. Another is manifest function that is intended to help some part of the societal system. In an ancillary way, the sociologist gives thought to and about latent function and unintended good consequences, as well as latent dysfunction and unintended bad consequences. When crises arise, and they will, this is part of the analyses by which counsel is constructed and offered.

In 2015 article in *Psychology Today,* a broad view of dealing with dysfunction was presented. It included:

Psychologists, generally define dysfunction in an individual that they associate with distress or impairment and a reaction that is not culturally expected. When considering if something is a symptom of a disorder. Consider the three Ds:
*(1) Is it psychologically **dysfunctional**?*
*(2) Is it **distressing** or result in it becoming a handicap to an individual or others?*
*(3) Is it associated with a response that is atypical or **deviant**?*
Psychological dysfunction refers to the cessation of purposeful functioning of cognition, emotions or behavior.

Memories play a large part of what enters into the thought patterns and lifestyle of a person. If the focus is on the mind, there would be an exploration of what the person is thinking now, and what influences of the past are latent (hidden or concealed) within the person. There is a tension between the human and spiritual factors. If one was reared in a home where there were certain rules but no sound rationale as to why these were rules being imposed, at the very least that person will be confused, maladjusted and most likely dysfunctional. Sadly, millions of people are suffering from chronic worry, hypertension, prejudice, guilt, hatred, fear, and sense of failure. Their condition and situation is due to that which has remained latent within one throughout his/her life. The concept of any part of the fruit of the Spirit (Galatians 5:22-23) governing one's reality has been elusive, especially regarding love, joy and peace. The person who has had little or no exposure to agape love has difficulty knowing and exhibiting true love. The same is true with true joy. The person may have moments where there has been the experience of happiness but it is short-lived once one returns into a home and atmosphere where the joy that originates with Jesus Christ is absent. It should not be surprising that peace is just a word rather than an ongoing experience. One's inner experience is one of turmoil rather than contentment, rest and freedom from anxiety.

A person can grow into teen and adult years handicapped by the absence of those things that would nurture a functional mind, emotion and will. The impact of the dysfunction can be seen in one's countenance and expressions of sorrow. There is usually the presence of anxiety, worry, strain and indecision. Another side effect of a chronic dysfunctional background is one's propensity toward physical maladies such as headaches, ulcers, high blood pressure, chest pains, and sundry other maladies imagined or real.

Memories are one of those things one cannot escape. A picture of my wife and I was posted on Facebook and received many nice comments. One acquaintance that I first knew more than 60 years ago, wrote a comment that inferred a negative memory. He wrote: "I was going to talk about college and seminary days but after reading the so affirmative comments about your lives lived and the impact you have had on others all I can say is look at you. What a great testimony to God's goodness to us all." Knowing and remembering this person as I do, my response was: "Hmmm - forgetting the things that are behind is a virtue, methinks. Sanctification is a process or refinement for all of us. We live with the reality of " IF ONLY" we would've known more and been mentored earlier

Becoming A Servant

in our lives. BUT GOD has His way and His purpose as He shapes us into who and what He wants us to be."

All of us have acquaintances that surface from time to time. They haven't had the opportunity of knowing one in the present. All they have is the baggage of their memories, accurate or exaggerated, from 50 or more years ago. Is it fair to view another person that way? No! Is it fair for a remote acquaintance from years ago to bring up his impressions that may be true or false? No! If the action of Jesus Christ's acceptance of a person just as they were was the practice of professing Christians today, what a difference it would make in our world. After all, this is the stated purpose and application of Romans 15:7 (NLT), "Accept each other just as Christ has accepted you so that God will be given glory."

Spiritual transitions can and will take place in one's life. Whether it is referenced as sanctification or spiritual growth, change will take place. This is basic if servanthood is to be maximized in one's life. A servant must be subservient to his master. The servant is to emulate his master. How can one be certain that this is occurring? Words written by Paul in Philippians 1:6, "a good work has been begun in you" and also the words in Philippians 2:13 (NLT), "God is working in you, giving you the desire and the power to do what pleases him." Paul also addresses the mind that one should gain and utilize. Philippians 2:5 (NIV), "In your relationships with one another, have the same mindset as Christ Jesus." When I was doing Pastoral Ministry, I visited with a woman who was advancing in years and asked her what Scripture verse was most meaningful to her. Without hesitancy, she quoted Second Timothy 1:7 (KJV), "God hath not given us the spirit of fear; but of power, and of love, and of a sound mind." When she arrived at the last phrase, she paused and held a finger alongside her temple and repeated, "a sound mind - a sound mind." What Scripture verse is most meaningful for you? How do you see yourself in terms of the servanthood specified by Jesus Christ, the Master?

There is always a time and place for the acceptance of the truth stated in Philippians 3:13-15 (NLT), "I focus on this one thing: Forgetting the past and looking forward to what lies ahead, I press on to reach the end of the race and receive the heavenly prize for which God, through Christ Jesus, is calling us. Let all who are spiritually mature agree on these things." Is this your focus and commitment? Do your acquaintances from the past believe and practice this commitment? What about your fellow-Christians in the present? How do they know you? What do they ascertain about you? Are you a good and faithful servant of Jesus Christ?

The words of a Hymn written in 1898 by Johnson Oatman, Jr. summarize the new goal and aspiration of the follower of Jesus Christ. Do these words give expression to who and what you are? Make these words an increasing reality in and for your life – starting now!

I'm pressing on the upward way,
New heights I'm gaining every day;
Still praying as I'm onward bound,
Lord, plant my feet on higher ground.

My heart has no desire to stay
Where doubts arise and fears dismay;
Though some may dwell where those abound,
My prayer, my aim, is higher ground.

Refrain:
Lord, lift me up and let me stand,
By faith, on Heaven's table land,
A higher plane than I have found;
Lord, plant my feet on higher ground.

13. Nuance and Innuendo

My beloved brothers, understand this: Everyone should be quick to listen, slow to speak, and slow to anger, for man's anger does not bring about the righteousness that God desires. Therefore, get rid of all moral filth and every expression of evil, and humbly receive the word planted in you, which can save your souls. Be doers of the word, and not hearers only. Otherwise, you are deceiving yourselves.
James 1:19-22

An adage asserts: "What you are speaks so loud I can't hear what you say." These words, or variants of them, have been attributed to Ralph Waldo Emerson. *The Quote Investigator* credits this concept to a publication written by Emerson (1876), *Letters and Social Aims*. In that writing, the following has been gleaned:

> *Let us not look east and west for materials of conversation, but rest in presence and unity. A just feeling will fast enough supply fuel for discourse, if speaking be more grateful than silence. When people come to see us, we foolishly prattle, lest we be inhospitable. But things said for conversation are chalk eggs (small talk). Don't say things. What you are stands over you the while, and thunders so that I cannot hear what you say to the contrary.*

The author of this review, Richard Bloch (July 2013) adds:

> *There's so much more drama in these words ...the ones that Emerson actually wrote. It's true. What you are does thunder so loudly that it creates dissonance with whatever you happen to be saying.*

Dissonance refers to lack of harmony or something that is discordant. Syllogistically, the dissonant postulate prevents a logical formulation or conclusion.

A valid point is that one's manner of life can project an image to others, rightly or wrongly, that allows an interpretation which may not be correct. Bluster does not always create reasonable and well-thought concepts that others can embrace and with which there will be a broad consensus of agreement. Also, body language, such as a person's gait, can project a portrait of insecurity or self-centeredness. A person's speech, vocabulary and grammar can project that one is lacking in knowledge and/or has developed a speech pattern designed to positively impress an audience. Obviously, there are people whose intellect is well known and whose spoken words result as a natural flow based upon one's study, education and skill sets. Also obvious, are those who are unwilling to strive for excellence in their use of vocabulary or grammar.

There are some professions, such as spokespersons or representatives, where being dubious is deemed to be normal and appropriate. One area where this is becoming increasingly prominent is in conversations or responses about issues by politicians. Do they represent their constituents or themselves? Are they influenced in their political speech by special interests/lobbyists or by that which is constitutionally correct? It results in one thinking and suggesting that politicians collectively are expressing what is characterized as "hot air" or conclusions that are incorrect. They project by their bloviation that they believe they are a person/persons of significant importance or knowledge. Someone once allowed that some people keep on speaking until they can think of something to say. Another way of considering meaningless speech or action is the expression that "a hollow log makes the most noise."

Within the Christian community and Church in general, there is the possibility of hypocrisy rather than reality

being the dominant construct. A devotional, *Today In The Word* – July 16, 2018 contained the observation:
> *A study by members of the Yale University psychology department found that people disdain hypocrisy for a reason other than the stigma of failing to practice what one preaches. People hate hypocrisy because false moralizing seems to be signaling the hypocrite's virtue. In any of our hypocritical beliefs or acts, we want others to see us as the one who is right on the issue in question. As much as hypocritical virtue brings contempt from other people, it brings far more contempt from the Lord, who sees right through our words and deeds to our true motives, intensions, and goals.*

The concluding statement, "it brings far more contempt from the Lord" was relevant during the earthly ministry of Jesus Christ. Hypocrisy is consistently viewed as the object of disdain in the contemporary church and other religious movements. In Matthew 23:13-16, 23, 25, 27, 29, Jesus is very clear about His view of hypocrisy. He speaks about it in a collective way, "Woe to you scribes and Pharisees, you hypocrites." He proceeds with a long list of areas where hypocrisy has dominated the lifestyle and influence of people who dominated the religious scene in their day. Woe is a term that is used fifty-five times in Scripture. The term needs to be understood as God intends. It is a pronouncement of judgment in Revelation 9 through 12. In the Gospels, Jesus used it to signify impending doom, condemnation and the wrath of God upon all hypocrites and their hypocrisies.

The perceived prevalence of hypocrisy may be one of the latent causes explaining why millennials have distanced themselves from organized and traditional religious groups. Are they anti-Christian? No! Do they hate the Jesus of the Gospel? No! Do they feel they are irrelevant in organized religion? Yes!

In April 2017, CBN News raised the issue and concern about millennials and their evolving attitude about the Christian religion. The CBN report begins with an observation:
Millennials are leaving church at record numbers and they are described as America's least religious generation. But while they may be highly skeptical of religion, they are still thirsty to find meaning in life. Studies show it isn't Jesus they're rejecting, they're rejecting churches that aren't making themselves relevant to Millennial culture.

This statement should be taken to heart. Tradition is dominating many church groups whether or not it is relevant to community or people's needs. The older leaders of the traditionally-oriented church need to take a look at what is happening within their community and congregation. The question they should ask themselves: Are we meeting genuine needs and caring about people's hurts in the present tense? Sadly, the answer in too many traditional, and especially in rural churches, is that existence is more of the focus rather than a ministry that adapts to the current demographic changes and ongoing needs/hurts of people within the changing demographic.

The CBN News report continues: "Researcher and president of LifeWay Christian Resources, Thom Rainer, says three things matter the most to Millennials: content, authenticity, and quality." Ironically, aren't these the same things people of all generations need to be concerned about in the same way? Thom Rainer goes on in his analysis and expands on what millennials want the most:

They Want Rich Content.
While many churches think they need flashing lights and a worship concert to attract the younger generation, that is simply not true. Millennials want a worship service that is contemplative and theologically

rich. They desire to sing those songs that reflect deep biblical and theological truth...Their focus is on theologically rich music. Millennials also want their churches to clearly communicate these theological truths through strategic signage and other means.
***They Want Authenticity*.**
Millennials can sense when the worship leaders and congregants are just going through the motions and they will quickly leave.
***They Want a Good Quality Worship Service*.**
Millennials want to attend a church service that shows the leaders put time and effort into making it run smoothly. They aren't looking for a show, they're looking for dedication and excellence. That quality is a reflection of the authenticity and is something any church can learn how to do.

Millennials are not rejecting Jesus, they are rejecting a coloration, a cultural adaptation, of Jesus that does not fit them...The answer IS Jesus. Millennials must see through culture, community, church, and family, to the Person who will never ignore them - Jesus.

Did hypocrites in Jesus' day project traditional function rather than contemporary relevance? Yes! Did they ignore the potential and possibility of being engaged in the Gospel pertaining to Jesus Christ and the role He wanted to have in people's lives? Yes! In a broader sense, can people other than Scribes and Pharisees be guilty of hypocrisy such as those upon whom the woes pronounced by Jesus Christ will be manifest? Yes! The question should not be thought of as rhetorical but one of perception. The fact is that some professing Christians are identified by Jesus Christ as being hypocrites upon whom God's judgment will come (See: Matthew 7:21-23 – "Not everyone saying Lord, Lord will enter the kingdom of heaven…").

A statement that needs to be carefully and consistently applied in one's life is James 4:16-17,
> You ought to say: If the Lord is willing, we will live and do this or that. As it is, you boast in your proud intentions. All such boasting is evil. therefore, whoever knows the right thing to do, yet fails to do it, is guilty of sin.

These words serve as an analysis of hypocrisy and how easily one can slide into being a hypocrite. When one allows boasting about who one is and what one thinks and does - this is hypocrisy. Actually that's being a braggart. Hypocrisy is boasting about oneself and then doing/being the opposite thing out of the spotlight. Do as I say, not as I do. It is usurping the authority of Jesus Christ in one's life and setting one's own standards and values as the measure of one's life. A real and present danger in James 4:16-17, as well as James 1:19-22, is that words and motives, innuendo and nuance are tolerated or misconstrued as being acceptable rather than being identified (which they so often are) as sin. Sometimes the inflection or tone of one's voice conveys a greater meaning and interpretation of the words that have been spoken. Innuendo is an indirect statement about a person or thing that is usually disparaging or being derogatory in form and intent. If someone was referred to as being a "blunderbuss" (a clumsy, unsubtle and insensitive person) – what would that suggest and convey to you? What conclusion would you arrive at after hearing that characterization? Nuance is a subtle difference or distinction in expression, meaning and/or response. Most of the time, either innuendo or nuance is deliberately employed rather than accidently occurring. When this is the case, denying or pretending it is not so, qualifies it as being sin, lying and hypocrisy. The use of either innuendo or nuance has an objective in view. It can be a dismissive statement or desires to affect your conclusion about a person or matter of concern. An example of innuendo or nuance can occur in a routine way. The name of a particular person can be given. Someone present could express, "Oh, him!" or "Oh, her." Absent is the basic consideration that raises practical questions one should have in mind before any response is given or any inflection, nuance or innuendo is utilized. One should ask : Is my expression kind, necessary and true? Either one of the expressions can conjure up all kinds of conclusions. More than likely it would convey or infer a negative impression and indicate that a person is unreliable; unacceptable; insensitive; lazy; not focused; etc.

When our children were very young, a chorus they were taught to sing was the *Be Careful* song. While it referenced all kinds of things that are said or done, one section emphasized: "Be careful little mouth what you say...for the Father up above is looking down." He is observing what one's tongue speaks; hands do; mind thinks; feet go. The prudent parent will add instruction based upon the words of Jesus Christ recorded in Matthew 12:36-37, "Everyone will give an account for every careless word spoken." A paraphrase rendering is: "Every idle word you speak." If there is application for the child, and there is, how much greater is the application for adults who might allow themselves to gossip, exaggerate, boast, bloviate, and demand from others response and behavior that they do not act upon or practice themselves.

In 1872, Frances R. Havergal wrote the words for focus, prayer and commitment: *Lord, Speak To Me*. Some of the stanzas are:

> *Lord, speak to me that I may speak*
> *In living echoes of Thy tone;*
> *As Thou has sought, so let me seek*
> *Thine erring children lost and lone.*

James Perry

O teach me, Lord, that I may teach
The precious things Thou dost impart;
And wing my words, that they may reach
The hidden depths of many a heart.

O give Thine own sweet rest to me,
That I may speak with soothing power
A word in season, as from Thee,
To weary ones in needful hour.

O fill me with Thy fullness, Lord,
Until my very heart overflow
In kindling thought and glowing word,
Thy love to tell, Thy praise to show.

    Are your words and actions free of hypocrisy, innuendo and nuance? Are you fastidious in your commitment to be like Jesus and to adequately represent Him? Are you a servant (follower) of your Master, the Lord Jesus Christ? May the song and goal of your heart be:

To be like Jesus,
To be like Jesus,
All I want, to be like Him,
His Presence fills me,
His love overwhelms me,
All I want, to be like Him.

To be like Jesus,
To be like Jesus!
My desire - to be like Him!
All through life's journey,
From earth to glory,
My desire - to be like Him.

14. Practicing Patience

We live in such a way that no one will stumble because of us, and no one will find fault with our ministry...We patiently endure troubles and hardships and calamities of every kind...We prove ourselves by our purity, our understanding, our patience, our kindness, by the Holy Spirit within us, and by our sincere love.
Second Corinthians 6:3-6 (NLT)

Servanthood and patience! Are they compatible with each other? Can a servant overcome resentment, frustration and lack of personal rights? Can a servant become one who is patient and diligent? Can a servant surrender his/her will to the will of a master? The answer is, Yes! However, it will take a lifetime of discipline, practice, diligence and development. At times when one needs to display patience, it seems to be elusive and impatience surfaces. I recall someone praying: "Lord! If you're trying to teach me patience, I have learned that lesson. Can we just get to Your answer for my prayer?" Dictionaries supply one with a variety of meanings for patience – what it means and how it should be enacted. Patience is: "Loss of temper, the bearing of provocation, annoyance, suppression of restlessness or annoyance when confronted with and having to deal with inordinate delay, steady perseverance, irritation, tempered care and diligence." Synonyms include: "calmness, stability, composure, persistent courage in trying circumstances, endurance, stoicism."

In Psychology Today, Dr. Judith Orloff writes about emotional freedom. In an article, *The Power of Patience,* Dr. Orloff writes:

Patience is a coping skill. Frustration is not the key to any door. Patience is a lifelong spiritual practice as well as a way to find emotional freedom. Frustration happens. Every day, there are plenty of good reasons to be impatient, such as, another long line; telemarketers; a goal not materializing fast enough; people don't do what they are supposed to do; rejection; disappointment. How is one to deal with it all? You can drive yourself crazy, behave irritably, feel victimized, or try to force an outcome – all are self-defeating reactions that alienate others and bring out the worst in them.

Or – you can learn to transform frustration with patience. Patience doesn't mean passivity or resignation, but power. It's an emotionally freeing practice of waiting, watching and knowing when to act.

Where are you when it comes to the display and practice of patience? Do you have it? Do you display it at all times? Do people see you as kind and caring, or as one who is a complainer and irritable because things aren't going the way you want them to go? I was taken by the phrasing Dr. Orloff used: "You can learn to transform frustration with patience." Transformation is a vital part of a Biblical Christian's relationship with Jesus Christ. Romans 12:2 uses the term, "Do not be conformed…but be transformed by the renewing of your mind."

Hebrews 10:36 (NKJV - ASV) instructs us: "For you have need of patience, that, after you have done the will of God, you might receive the promise." In other translations, an alternative for patience is: persevere (NIV), endurance (NLT; ESV). All are stating a corresponding truth that to gain patience, one will have to learn to persevere and develop endurance. It is important to link these words together because God's response to one's prayer is that one may receive His promise that it will happen. However, the Lord does not always indicate when it will happen.

Becoming A Servant

An example is Genesis 17:1-6, 17 where Abraham and Sarah are promised an heir, a son. God established a covenant with them: "I am God almighty; walk before me and be blameless, that I...may multiply you greatly." What would this covenant mean and when would it be enacted? God did not say and Abraham did not know. How should one proceed with a promise of God, especially when one is advance in years. Abraham was 99 years of age. Sarah was 10 years younger. Abraham's response to God's covenant is given in Genesis 17:17 (NASB), "Abraham fell on his face and laughed. He said in his heart: will a child be born to a man 100 years old? And will Sarah, who is 90 years old, bear a son?"

Laughter was a first response to God's covenant promise. Later, Sarah would also laugh at the prospect of pregnancy and motherhood. Their response did not go unnoticed by God. When their son is finally born, God told them to name him – Isaac (which means: laughter). It would serve as a constant reminder that God is always faithful to His Word. That which He has promised, He will do. In His way and in His timeframe, His promise will be fulfilled and His people will rejoice. A cautionary word is appropriate when one is waiting for God's promise to be actuated. Abraham and Sarah became impatient waiting for the promised son and heir. Sarah devised an alternate plan to God's promise and purpose. She told Abraham that he should wait no longer but to go into her much younger Egyptian maid, Hagar and use her to produce that which God had promised Genesis 16 and 21. Was that a good move? Was it God's will for them? The answer to both questions is, No! Hagar did conceive and give birth to a son whom she named, Ishmael. After he had reached his teen years, Sarah insisted that Hagar be sent away into the wilderness. Jewish tradition believes that Ishmael became the forefather to a number of Bedouin peoples dwelling in Southern Palestine. Several commentaries allow that the descendants of Ishmael are the Arabs who have become a perpetual source of tension with the Jews and Israel.

Impatience, or taking matters into one's own hands, is never a suitable alternative to God's promise and will. Waiting will require an unrestrictive time-frame if one is to glean, learn and implement Biblical patience in one's personal life. One must remember who he/she is as a follower of Jesus Christ. This is necessary to understand God's ramifications for servanthood.

Servanthood lessons one must learn are shared in Psalm 37:1-8 (NKJV).

Lesson 1: Do not fret and do not be envious.

Lesson 2: Trust in the Lord and do good.

Lesson 3: Delight yourself in the Lord alone. As a benefit for having done so – He will give you the desires of your heart.

Lesson 4: Commit your way – the direction of your life – to the Lord and trust Him implicitly.

Lesson 5: Rest in the Lord and wait patiently for His direction for you.

Lesson 6: Don't compare yourself to others, especially those who are secular in their lifestyle, or fret because of their prosperity versus your perceived poverty.

Lesson 7: Don't let anger or wrath become your obsession or it will result in your downfall. These principles for life and guidelines for spiritual character are sometimes difficult to faithfully implement.

When I wrote and published the book, *The Journey Along The Narrow Way*, there was a passing reference to practicing patience as a servant of the Lord. Frustration can interfere with patience. The sense of fairness and equanimity can fester into resentment and negative expressions. Decisions and choices can be an impediment when the servant wants to consistently practice patience. I wrote:

Becoming A Servant

Jesus Christ made a distinction between The Narrow Pathway and the Broad Way. In the Sermon on the Mount, Matthew 7:13-14 (BSB – Berean Study Bible), Jesus said: Enter through the narrow gate. For wide is the gate and broad is the way that leads to destruction, and many enter through it. But small is the gate and narrow the way that leads to life, and only a few find it. When Jesus indicated that only a few find the narrow way, He is indicating that individual discipline and commitment are vital to one both finding the narrow way and continuing on it. Admittedly, there will be distractions that occur where choices must be made. At such a moment, do I continue along this narrow way even though it is difficult to do, or will I allow myself to determine an alternative that is less rigid?

Will my choice keep me on the narrow way, or will a lesser general consensus become my alternative choice?

What will occur if I choose the path of my alternative choice? What will distract me and entice me to turn from the narrow way focus and commitment? I wrote the following:

In desperate and challenging times, people who are more steeped in traditions or superstitions will begin to pray to anything or anyone as they seek for and want relief or deliverance from a situation that is marginal or with which one is incapable of coping. This is a reason why so many world-wide continue to pray to gods of their own making and choosing – idols, martyrs, saints (so-designated). They hope that their repetitious recitations, incantations, and obeisance to some tradition or ritual will somehow bring about a desired result. It is not dissimilar to a good-luck orientation and practice – clinging to four-leaf clovers, rabbit's feet, beads, medals and/or medallions.

How does the Lord view one's rituals, traditions, customs, incantations and self-made idols? There is an interesting situation described in Ezekiel 14:1-8. Some of the elders in Israel come to the prophet to seek His wisdom and God's direction and blessing for the people. The Lord instructs the prophet to state a singular focus regarding the present need of the people. The Lord declares and poses the question (verse 3): "Son of man, these men have set up idols in their hearts and put wicked stumbling blocks before their faces. Should I let them inquire of me at all?" The phrase that should cause soul-searching is: "idols in their hearts." Some of those idols are pride, lust, envy, spirit of strife, self-will – all kinds of things that are common to the carnal person but cannot be present in the spiritual person.

What does the Lord convey is the only thing he will entertain on behalf of the people and their representatives? Why does he disallow anything they wish to express to Him? Is there any way they will be able to communicate with the living God? Is there any action they will have to take? Any amends they will have to make? The answer and message for the people from the Lord is given in Verse 6, "This is what the Sovereign Lord says: Repent! Turn from your idols and renounce all your detestable practices!" This is God's response to all people in all generations. On a day when Jesus was ministering to a mixed group of religiously-oriented people, He stated (Luke 13:5), "I tell you…unless you repent, you too will all perish." This message would be echoed and proclaimed on the day of Pentecost as Peter preached a message that resulted in conviction among the people. Acts 2:37-38 records, "When the people heard this, they were cut to the heart and said to Peter and the other apostles: Brothers, what shall we do? Peter replied: Repent!" Anything less than one repenting will prevent one being or becoming a servant of the Lord.

Becoming A Servant

How does one realize all of what new life in Jesus Christ means? Will the one who is to be a disciple of Jesus Christ experience spiritual growth immediately? No! There is a perspective about God and His way of calling a people to Himself that needs to be understood. What are His qualities and characteristics? In Isaiah 30, there is a twofold perspective one needs to observe about God.

First, in verse 15, *"This is what the Sovereign Lord, the Holy One of Israel, says: In repentance and rest is your salvation, in quietness and trust is your strength, but you would have none of it."*

Second, in verse 18, *"Yet the Lord longs to be gracious to you; therefore he will rise up to show you compassion. For the Lord is a God of justice. Blessed are all who wait (patiently) for him!"*

For one to become a servant of the Lord and be enabled to represent Him effectively, repentance is an absolute requirement. To learn about His will and way for one's life will require patiently waiting upon the Lord. The prayer one should always be willing to express is:

Make me a servant, Humble and meek…
And may the prayer Of my heart always be…
Make me a servant today.

15. Decisions

Teach me Your way, O Lord, and I will walk in Your truth. Grant me undividedness of heart so that I may fear Your name. I will praise You, O Lord my God, with all my heart; I will glorify Your name forever. For great is Your loving devotion to me; You have delivered me…
Psalm 86:11-13

One of the values in reading the Word of God each day is to gain a heart for the things of God and to anticipate being in His presence in a personal and devoted way. I believe the Lord uses His Word to remind each one of truths that should never be forgotten. In a devotional time, I was reading Psalm 86 and verses 11-13 gripped my heart and thoughts.

Teach me your way, O Lord, that I may walk in your truth; unite my heart to fear your name. I give thanks to you, O Lord my God, with my whole heart, and I will glorify your name forever. For great is your steadfast love toward me; you have delivered my soul from the depths of hell.

David recognized his personal need and prayed that God would intervene on his behalf. His petition has three key components.

First is David's desire for the Lord to teach him God's way and will. When praying, he makes the commitment to respond obediently and walk in His truth.

Second is David's plea that the Lord would grant him undividedness of heart. His motivation was that he might learn more completely to fear the name of the Lord.

Third his desire and petition pertains to praise and glory that will be directed to the Lord alone. The intensity of his commitment is that he would praise the Lord with all his heart and that he would glorify the name of the Lord forever. Why did he have this sensitivity and level of commitment? Simply, David recognized the greatness of the Lord's loving devotion to him.

Matthew Henry Concise Commentary on Psalm 86:7-17 shares the following thoughts:

> *Our God alone possesses almighty power and infinite love. Christ is the way and the truth. And the believing soul will be more desirous to be taught the way and the truth. And the believing soul will be more desirous to be taught the way and the truth of God, in order to walk therein, than to be delivered out of earthly distress. Those who set not the Lord before them, seek after believers' souls; but the compassion, mercy, and truth of God, will be their refuge and consolation…In considering David's experience, and that of the believer, we must not lose sight of Him, who though he was rich, yet for our sakes He became poor, that we through His poverty might become rich.*

The petition that pierces my own heart and commitment is the desire of David for undividedness of heart. He knew that his usefulness for the Lord as King would require his own personal oneness with Him. It is consistent with a prayer that Jesus would offer for His disciples and followers in John 17:20-21.

> *I am not asking on behalf of them alone, but also on behalf of those who will believe in Me through their message, that all of them may be one, as You, Father, are in Me, and I am in You. May they also be in Us, so that the world may believe that You sent Me.*

Undividedness of heart and oneness with those of like precious faith is not for personal satisfaction alone but so that

Becoming A Servant

there would be a credible impact in the world in which they lived, served and ministered. The servant must radiate the qualities of the Master so that the message of the Gospel will impact the greatest number of people throughout the world. Another part of Jesus' prayer is His desire for His followers (V. 13), "that they may have My joy fulfilled within them." It echoes a premise and fact that in the ebb and flow of life there is joy in serving Jesus.

For many years one of my Biblical heroes has been Caleb. The uniqueness of the life and commitment of Caleb is that he is always referenced as one who followed the Lord wholeheartedly. He never swerved away from his commitment and utilized all of his personal energy to make certain that the will and purpose of God would be realized for God's people as they entered and settled in the promised land. For a good portion of my life, my prayer and hope has been that I might be remembered as Caleb was throughout his life. Simply, it is that he followed the Lord wholeheartedly. I am attracted to the words he expressed in Joshua14:6-12, where he references that he and Joshua were the only spies who had followed the Lord wholeheartedly. He recalls and rehearses the promise of Moses about inheritances in the promised land when Caleb was forty years of age. For the next forty-five years h Caleb assisted the other tribes to get settled in their designated homeland. He is now ready to inherit his mountain. His appeal to Joshua is given in verse 9: (At age eighty-five, he said): "I am still as strong today as I was in the day that Moses sent me; my strength now is as my strength was then…So now, give me my mountain (hill country) of which the Lord spoke on that day. I am well able to conquer it."

These similar words of both David and Caleb about "undividedness of heart" and "followed the Lord wholeheartedly" resonate in my heart, soul and mind.

In 1857, Horatius wrote:
Thy way, not mine, O Lord,

James Perry

However dark it be!
Lead me by Thine own hand,
Choose out the path for me.

Smooth let it be or rough,
It will be still the best;
Winding or straight, it leads
Right onward to Thy rest.

Not mine, not mine the choice
In things or great or small;
Be Thou my guide, my strength
My wisdom, and my all.

    Servanthood and subservience requires that one conforms to the Master's will for one's life. How does one ascertain the will of the Lord for one's life? For some, making or reaching a decision seems to be easy. How they reach a decision is another matter. Some are ego-driven and have a spirit of being superior to others. Others are hesitant, rightly or wrongly, as they feel a sense of inadequacy, inferiority or unworthiness. The Biblical words of caution should always be primary for everyone. Proverbs 16:2 (BSB) is a good cautionary reminder: "All a man's ways are pure in his own eyes, but his motives are weighed by the Lord." Just think – one's motives being weighed by the Lord. Proverbs 14:15 (NASB) reminds one: "The naive believes everything, But the sensible man considers his steps." The wise and sensible person considers carefully what steps should be taken and what decisions should be made. Will it be easy and simple? No! Will it require patience in prayer? Yes! Will the Lord be the trusted guide whose guidance you are seeking? Yes! The words that are helpful are expressed in Isaiah 30:21 (BSB), "And whether you turn to the right or to the left, your ears will hear this command behind you: "This is the way. Walk in it."

Becoming A Servant

Do you listen for that still small voice of the Lord? Is your ear attuned to detect His whisper to you? Do you want to know His way and the pathway you should take? That's where I want to be. That's where you should want to be. That's where the Biblical Church needs to be. Is that where you/we are today?

I also want the words of Abraham's servant as he travelled to find a bride for Isaac to be true for me. How would he know where to go? How would he be enabled to make the right and wise decision on behalf of his Master? The words in Genesis 24:27 (KJV) state the answer: "I being in the way, the Lord led me." When I was eighteen years old, The Selective Service of the United States was drafting young men to serve in the military. The Korean War, while nearing an armistice, was continuing and military personnel were needed. I received a notice to appear for a physical examination and was classified as 1-A. It was advised that one's employer be notified of the possibility that one could be drafted and would report for military service within the next thirty days. This was done and a replacement was found to assume my employment position. Thirty days came and went. No draft notice was received. No longer having employment, I volunteered to assist at a Bible Camp in upstate New York. During my younger years, I had attended this camp.

When the summer drew to a close and the camp was closing, some friends I had made were enrolled in Columbia Bible College in Columbia, South Carolina. They invited me to ride with them and then I could hitchhike back home. We drove there in a yellow Mercury convertible and stopped at swimming pools along the way. All I had with me was my bathing suit and a towel. When we arrived in Columbia, there was a time for orientation and I sat in those sessions with my friends. I was handed some of the orientation forms but was dismissive of them. However, afterwards, a staff member asked me about enrollment as a student. I told him I was waiting for my draft notice and really had no plans of attending any college. I told him that I had no clothes with me and no money to pay for tuition or room and board. But then, the staff member posed one of those inescapable questions: "If we pray with you for the Lord's provision for your tuition, room and board, would you be willing to enroll as a student?" I don't remember "why" but I do remember almost instantly answering yes.

How does the Lord get a person who has a pending draft notice to serve in the nation's military into a calling to serve the Lord anywhere, at any-time, in any place and at any cost? In retrospect, I can understand His plan and fitting my life into it. What was His plan for my life? I enrolled in school in September 1954. I was preparing to be drafted and called by the United States Government to serve in the army. However, the Lord was preparing me to be called by Him to serve Him wherever He would lead me. Little did I realize that His plan would include the enrollment in January 1955 of a godly and beautiful young woman whom He had chosen to be my life partner in ministry. After we were married in June 1956, we had thoughts of becoming missionaries and serving Him in China. That door was closed as missionaries were expelled from that land by the Communist government. We were willing to adapt and to serve the Chinese-speaking people who had escaped and migrated out of China to other smaller nations. We began preliminary applications but it soon became apparent that the Lord wanted us to serve Him in the local church.

Would that be an easy assignment? Would there be times when we would have to depend fully upon Him for His provisions for us and our family? Would these times have a negative or positive impact upon our children? There were two Biblical passages that Peggy and I had taken together as our life commitment – Hebrews 12:2 and Psalm 37:4, 5 and 7a.

Becoming A Servant

From those early days until later life, the verses we have claimed are in Psalm 37:23-26 (NLT),

> *The Lord directs the steps of the godly. He delights in every detail of their lives. Though they stumble, they will never fall, for the Lord holds them by the hand. Once I was young, and now I am old. Yet I have never seen the godly abandoned or their children begging for bread. The godly always give generous loans to others, and their children are a blessing.*

The one called by the Lord to be His servant will be committed to His will, His way and His timing for his life. This is valid for the husband and wife who have jointly been called to serve Him. It will require of them and their family to learn more about the ways of the Lord and to always wait patiently upon Him. In 1875, Fanny Crosby wrote words that are useful as an expression of one's desire and commitment. The servants who are subservient want to continue to follow and walk in the way of their Master. They find pleasure in the truth and reality of the words:

> *All the way my Savior leads me;*
> *O the fullness of His love!*
> *This my song through endless ages—*
> *Jesus led me all the way.*

If a change is made in the lyric from the singular to the plural, the words of purpose and testimony become,

> *All the way **OUR** Savior led **US**;*
> *O the fullness of His love!*
> *This **OUR** song through endless ages—*
> *Jesus led **US** all the way…*

To Him be the glory, Great Things He has done!

16. The Inescapable

And Hezekiah received the letter from the hand of the messengers, and read it; and Hezekiah went up to the house of the Lord, and spread it before the Lord. Then Hezekiah prayed to the Lord, saying: O Lord of hosts, God of Israel, the One who dwells between the cherubim. You are God, You alone, of all the kingdoms of the earth. You have made heaven and earth. Incline Your ear, O Lord, and hear; open Your eyes, O Lord, and see; and hear all the words of Sennacherib, which he has sent to reproach the living God.
Isaiah 37:14-17

    Learning to pray is a life-long journey of increasing one's faith and trusting the Lord implicitly. One needs to arrive at a point where prayer is a normal reflex on one's part. Regardless of the need, whether it is great or small, the Lord and His will and His guidance should be sought. There is nothing too large or too insignificant when it comes to one's walk of faith and trust in the Lord. He will provide the needed guidance. He will disclose His will and the right timing for it to be carried out. This reminds me of a gospel chorus from my youth: "The Lord knows the way through the wilderness; All I have to do is follow. Strength for today is mine always and all I need for tomorrow. My Lord knows…" He will also provide for one's need(s) as one asks, seeks and knocks on the heart of God for the particulars of life.

    There may be times in life when one is essentially trapped and in a dangerous situation. One is unaware that any reasonable alternative is available. The Bible records a military situation where the people of the Lord are surrounded by superior forces that want to eliminate them as a distinctive people. When all of the temporal factors indicate a secular, military threat and demand is at hand, what can be done? When there is no ally to appeal to for help, how can one face the superior force and obstacle? When all available manpower is prepared for battle and no reinforcements are in reserve, how can there be hope when reason for despair seems so obvious? When Saul and his army were frozen in place because they were frightened by the presence of the Philistines and their giant Goliath (First Samuel 17), what was their plan or resolve? Would they pray to the Lord and seek His aid? Would the Lord set His plan in motion for their deliverance and victory before they seek Him? The Lord had a plan and a man to carry it out. He will not use one who is paralyzed in fear. His man, David, will be bold and courageous. He will be confident because of His experience of the Lord's faithfulness when he was tending his father's sheep. He knew that God would make a way where there seemed to be no way just as God does for all who trust in Him.

It's easy to think that if the Christian community today had evidence of the presence of God, it would be much easier to live godly and righteous lives. Lives that would be undaunted by any negative human influences but would be lived confidently, boldly and victoriously. Do you believe that would be our reality and experience? Think about the exodus of God's people from their bondage in Egypt and their journey toward the promised land. If God's people in that day believed God knew what He was doing as evidenced by all they had experienced, their journey toward Jericho and the promised land would've been relatively short. However, because of their negativity, fears and disbelief, the original cadre of adult Israelites would never reach the promised land. They would wander for forty years and die in the wilderness. They had chosen to ignore the power of God displayed in the plagues. They disregarded the purpose and meaning of the blood on the doorposts of their homes and how it brought about deliverance for their firstborn male. They grumbled against Moses and their leaders; they complained about their food; they were discontent and thought about how much better things would be back in the land of bondage. They chose to be blind to the Shekinah cloud that led them by day and the pillar of fire that protected at night. Foolish thinking? Yes! Rebellious people? Yes!

One wonders how they could forget the moment when the Shekinah cloud led them to the shore of the Red Sea. Did they believe that God would enable them to get to the other side safely? No! Did they think about the power of God who brought them to this place and who would not fail them? No! All they could think about was the Egyptian army that had been pursuing them and were now closing in upon them. They saw the Red Sea as the place of death rather than a pathway to a new and better way of life. Their conclusion was that they were trapped and would be killed. They were in an inescapable predicament. Their leader had only a stick of wood. He could call it a staff or a rod of God but they saw it and believed it was only a branch from a tree. Eyes can so easily become blinded and ears so easily deafened to God and His Word.

At the appropriate time, Moses would extend his staff (stick) by the Red Sea. By God's power, the waters would stop their natural flow and heap up so a pathway to safety would be available to the people. With all of their cantankerous ways; with all of their fears and complaints; with all of their rebellion; they took advantage of this unforeseen way of escape and went through the Red Sea on dry ground. Scripture is very kind in its description of this moment. Hebrews 11:29 records: "By faith the people passed through the Red Sea as on dry land; but when the Egyptians tried to follow, they were drowned."

Have you ever found yourself in an inescapable situation? Have you felt trapped and thought your demise was imminent? What would you have done if you were on the journey to the promised land? What causes your halting and hesitating on your journey along the narrow way? What do you do when you are restricted by the mandates of Jesus Christ and the restrictions of the narrow way? Do you view these mandates and restrictions as an infringement of your personal liberty or as a protection against evil?

All of us have been in an inescapable situation and place. Paul summarizes it well in Ephesians 2:1-10. The inescapable was the fact of being dead in trespasses and sins. There was no human way to escape the clutches of the enemy of one's soul. One who is dead (spiritually) lacks any ability to act in his/her own behalf. The body, mind, soul and spirit were all held captive by spiritual forces of darkness. It would take an act of power to shatter the chains that bind one and to be set free indeed. How can the inescapable be overcome and freedom result from the captivity wherein one was found? There is a tremendous and powerful phrase used by Paul. It is, "But God." Ephesians 2:4-5 expresses: "But God, who is rich in mercy, made us alive with Christ even when we were dead in transgressions - it is by grace you have been saved." Peter also expresses it well (First Peter 1:3-5),

Praise be to the God and Father of our Lord Jesus Christ! In his great mercy he has given us new birth into a living hope through the resurrection of Jesus Christ from the dead, and into an inheritance that can never perish, spoil or fade. This inheritance is kept in heaven for you, who through faith are shielded by God's power until the coming of the salvation that is ready to be revealed in the last time.

God has made a way from the inescapable at just the right time in His Son, Jesus Christ. The words of Romans 5:6-8 remind one:

You see, at just the right time, when we were still powerless, Christ died for the ungodly. Very rarely will an-

yone die for a righteous person, though for a good person someone might possibly dare to die. But God demonstrates his own love for us in this: While we were still sinners, Christ died for us.

The text indicates that when we were powerless and held in the inescapable clutches of the evil one, God displayed His power and the chains fell off. He set us free and gave us new life and victory. You may be facing impossible and inescapable situations in your life. You may feel helpless and hopeless. You may be overwhelmed that the enemy is too powerful and your strength is inadequate and useless. But God, knows who you are and where you are. He has a perfect plan and purpose that He will carry out in His way and at His time. You can and should believe that God will make a way for you. To know that reality in your life, you must come to the living God and trust in Him. William T. Sleeper (1874) wrote:

Out of my bondage, sorrow, and night,
Jesus, I come, Jesus, I come.
Into Thy freedom, gladness, and light,
Jesus, I come to Thee.
Out of my sickness, into Thy health,
Out of my want and into Thy wealth,
Out of my sin and into Thyself,
Jesus, I come to Thee.

17. Amazement

The (paralytic) man stood up before them, took what he had been lying on, and went home glorifying God. Everyone was taken with amazement and glorified God. They were filled with awe and said, We have seen remarkable things today.
Luke 5:25-26

One of the important servanthood lessons the disciples learned was that Jesus could do amazing and powerful things in His ministry. Later on, before His ascension, He told the disciples to remain in Jerusalem until they received power when the Holy Spirit came upon them (Acts 1:8). As they continue to minister in His name, the power bestowed upon them would validate who they were serving and whose ministry they were continuing. On the Day of Pentecost, people who heard the servants of God minister (Acts 2:7-8),

...were amazed and were marveling, saying, Behold, are not all these who are speaking Galileans? And how do we each hear our own language in which we were born?

Others went further in their observations and in their hostility toward anything that represented Jesus Christ. Acts 2:12-13 (NIV) records the rejection and ridicule by some, "Amazed and perplexed, they asked one another, "What does this mean?" Some, however, made fun of them and said, "They have had too much wine." The apostles were undaunted and pressed on with their ministry calling and assignment. The message of amazing grace must be told and the real power of God must be made known.

Over the years, several books have been written that have in the title some expression about amazing grace. One tome is titled, *Amazed By Grace*. A review speaks of *Amazed By Grace* as being: "A divine enabling power that allows us to overcome weaknesses, accomplish things beyond our capacity, and become more Christlike than we ever could with our greatest personal effort." An example of Amazing Grace being practiced is John M. Perkins. A portion of his life story can be read in the book, *Let Justice Roll Down*. Even though he was subjected to abuse, suffering and indignity, he was enabled by God's grace to forgive the racial injustices he encountered in rural Mississippi. By God's grace, he has sought to help others to forgive the oppressors and to trust in God's goodness.

The idea of amazing grace is also shared in music. No one will soon forget the words so clearly and reflectively written by John Newton, "*Amazing Grace*, how sweet the sound that saved a wretch like me..." Throughout his journey in life, he was keenly aware of the amazing grace of an amazing God. In his life and after his death, he wanted that testimony to be known by all who research his life. His message was simply that God is merciful and His grace is unlimited.

Another hymn that many identify with conveys a general thought about amazing grace is, *My Savior's Love*. The words convey the special relationship and blessing one has in Jesus Christ.

I stand amazed in the presence
of Jesus the Nazarene;
And wonder how He could love me,
A sinner, condemned, unclean.
How marvelous! How wonderful!
And my song shall ever be...

How amazed are you as you reflect upon the grace and mercy of God?

Becoming A Servant

Paul did not have enough superlatives available when he wrote about the great love and grace of God, Ephesians 2:4-7,

> But because of **His great love** for us, God, who is **rich in mercy**, made us alive with Christ, even when we were dead in our trespasses. **It is by grace** you have been saved! God raised us up with Christ and seated us with Him in the heavenly realms in Christ Jesus, in order that in the coming ages He might display **the surpassing riches of His grace**, demonstrated by **His kindness** to us in Christ Jesus.

Paul continued to state in Ephesians 2 that salvation is all grace and apart from any human effort or works. He goes on to say in verse 10 that "good works" will become a vital part of the one who has been saved by grace: "For we are God's workmanship, created in Christ Jesus to do good works, which God prepared in advance as our way of life." One's new way of life in Christ will emanate works of righteousness and godliness.

Part of the amazing grace process involves the servant's learning to lean upon Jesus and all of His promises. We should never forget the truth expressed by Paul in Second Corinthians 1:20, "For all the promises of God are "Yes" in Christ. And so through Him, our "Amen" (Yes, so be it) is spoken to the glory of God." The *Dictionary of Bible Themes* documents that there are more than 5,467 divine promises within the Bible. One the many promises of God, is Isaiah 65:24, "Even before they call, I will answer, and while they are still speaking, I will hear." While these words are in an eschatological context, the words coordinate well with those spoken by Jesus Christ in The Sermon on the Mount. In Matthew 6:31-33 Jesus stated:

> *Do not worry, saying, What shall we eat? What shall we drink? What shall we wear? ...Your Heavenly Fa-*

ther knows that you need them...Seek first the kingdom of God and His righteousness, and all these things will be added unto you.

Jesus continues and shares the process and procedure for the enactment of this truth in Matthew 7:7-8,
Ask and it will be given to you; seek and you will find; knock and the door will be opened to you. For everyone who asks receives; he who seeks finds; and to him who knocks, the door will be opened.

The formulation makes an interesting mnemonic device for the word ASK. A = Ask; S = Seek and K = Knock. Devices are an easy way to remember what and how one is to approach God in Prayer. Another device that aids a servant well is The Hand illustration developed by The Navigators. The five fingers of the hand represent and remind one to have a daily plan for seeking God.
The Thumb = Hearing the Word of God (Romans 10:17);
The Forefinger = Reading the Word of God (Revelation 1:3);
The Middle Finger = Studying the Word of God (Acts 17:11);
The Ring Finger = Memorizing the Word of God (Psalm 119:9, 11); and
The Pinky = Meditating on the Word of God (Psalm 1:2-3).

By following these techniques and devices, one will begin to learn more of the promises of God and learn how to implement the promises in one's life.

In your personal relationship with Jesus Christ do you embrace, believe and practice His promises? Are you able to say and mean, Great is Your faithfulness, Lord unto me? Two personal truths that have come together for my wife and me are that God knows what our needs are and before we even call upon Him, He is answering, and before we are able to frame our requests, He has already heard. This causes us to continually be amazed by His marvelous grace.

Last week, we received a statement from one of the medical providers that I have seen since last November. The bill was dated December 2017. While it wasn't an amount as horrendous as it might've been, my response to my wife was: "This Doctor was so good and kind at a time when I was so much in need. But – how will we pay the amount?" The Lord promised He would provide and He did.

A Pastor who had surgery was unable to return to the Pulpit as he had hoped and I was asked to preach in his and the church's behalf. I was delighted to be able to say: "I will try my best and do what I can." That was followed by another invitation to lead the worship service with a very dear group of God's people. Both churches were gracious in giving an honorarium for the ministry effort. The total amount received was sufficient to cover the statement amount from last December.

Were we amazed by His grace and faithfulness? Emphatically, Yes! Had the Lord answered before we called upon Him in prayer? Again, emphatically, Yes!

On August 4, 2018, I was reading Our Daily Bread devotional and was struck by the title and content about *Radical Love* which included a special paragraph of a personal sadness and disappointment. The devotional tells a story about how one week prior to a woman's wedding date her engagement suddenly and abruptly ended. The devotional records that:

> Despite her sadness and disappointment, she decided not to waste the food she had purchased for her wedding reception. She changed the negative event into a positive ministry by revamping the guest list and inviting the residents of local homeless shelters to the feast.

Her generosity reflects Luke 14:13 where Jesus said: When you give a banquet, invite the poor, the crippled, the lame, the blind.

Jesus gave this instruction as He sat at a meal given by a Pharisee.

The Biblical Christian can sometimes be perplexed with the outworking of amazing grace. It does one well to remember the words in Isaiah 55:8-12 (NKJV),

My thoughts are not your thoughts, nor are your ways My ways, says the Lord. For as the heavens are higher than the earth, So are My ways higher than your ways, and My thoughts than your thoughts ....My word that goes forth from My mouth shall not return to Me void, but it shall accomplish what I please, and it shall prosper in the thing for which I sent it.

When endeavoring to understand the amazing grace of the amazing God, there are several phrases that should be indelibly traced in one's mind. The phrases spoken by the Lord for His people to note and remember are:

(1) My thoughts;
(2) My ways;
(3) My words;
(4) My mouth;
(5) It will accomplish what I please;
(6) (It will accomplish) the thing for which I sent it.

If we remember these things, it should free us from being afraid, alone, perplexed, anxious.

One must know and believe that the grace, mercy and love of God is always amazing. Because of this fact, we should marvel, as well as be amazed by His grace and faithfulness. We should never forget the words of Ephesians 3:20-21,

Becoming A Servant

Now to Him who is able to do infinitely more than all we ask or imagine, according to His power that is at work within us, to Him be the glory in the church and in Christ Jesus throughout all generations, forever and ever. Amen.

In 1918, Haldor Lillenas wrote the words to *Wonderful Grace of Jesus*. The hymn is based on the words in First Timothy 1:14 (NIV),

Wonderful grace of Jesus,
Greater than all my sin;
How shall my tongue describe it,
Where shall its praise begin?
Taking away my burden,
Setting my spirit free;
For the wonderful grace of Jesus
reaches me.
Refrain:
Wonderful the matchless grace of Jesus,
Deeper than the mighty rolling sea;
Higher than the mountain,
sparkling like a fountain,
All-sufficient grace for even me!
Broader than the scope of my transgressions,
Greater far than all my sin and shame;
Oh, magnify the precious Name of Jesus,
Praise His Name!

18. Astonishment

When He (Jesus) came in, He said to them, Why make this commotion and weep? The child is not dead, but sleeping. And they ridiculed Him (laughed Him to scorn – KJV). But when He had put them all outside, He took the father and the mother of the child, and Peter, James and John with Him, and entered where the child was lying. Then He took the child by the hand, and said: I say to you, arise. Immediately the girl arose and walked, for she was twelve years of age. And they were overcome with great amazement (astonished with a great astonishment – KJV).
Mark 5:39-42 (NKJV)

The definition for astonished/astonishment has multiple possibilities: "amazement; confusion of the mind from fear, surprise or admiration at an extraordinary or unexpected event." When searching the book listings on Amazon for any religious titles on this subject, there is only one significant tome listed: *Astonishing Grace* by Edwin S. Walker. This book references years of missionary activity in Haiti where people, especially men, who were deprived physically and denied culturally were transformed into servants of the Lord by the astonishing grace of God and through years of patient effort and mentoring by the missionary servant. Many unknown missionaries labor in unheard of places among people who speak various languages. Some of these places are politically volatile and can be dangerous. The missionaries go with courage to serve their Lord and Master, Jesus Christ. They share the commitment expressed by Paul in Acts 20:24,
> *But none of these things move me, neither count I my life dear unto myself, so that I might finish my course*

with joy, and the ministry, which I have received of the Lord Jesus, to testify the gospel of the grace of God.

How does one arrive at this point? What is the motivation to go to the unknown and unreached tribes and people throughout the world? I wonder if the words of the hymn, *Come, Thou Fount Of Every Blessing* have any bearing on their unwavering commitment? Consider,

*Come, Thou fount of every blessing,
Tune my heart to sing Thy grace…*

*Yet from what I do inherit,
Here Thy praises I'll begin…*

*O to grace how great a debtor
Daily I'm constrained to be!*

It is that sense of being constrained to be the servant Jesus Christ has called and compels one to go anywhere, to go at any time, to do any work, at any cost. The result of their labor in Christ's name will cause some to be astonished.

There aren't too many uses of the word astonished or astonishment in the Scriptures. There are inferences and illustrations of how the Lord worked in dramatic ways by His miraculous power and through the commitment and faith of His servants. Mark 5 has the account of Jairus coming to Jesus because of the great need of his daughter. While he waits to speak with Jesus, a messenger informs Jairus that his daughter has died. Jesus shares a personal word with Jairus (verse 36): "Don't be afraid. Just (only) believe." Will Jairus be able to heed these words amid this moment of shock and sorrow? Will the people who know him and his family encourage him to have confidence and trust in the words of Jesus Christ? How will they respond when they follow Jesus and Jairus to the home where the girl has died? What is the scene they will encounter? Verse 38, (KJV) indicates there was: "tumult, and them that wept and wailed greatly."

When Jesus arrives, He makes a statement that receives a negative response and derision. In Verse 39-40, Jesus asked, "Why do you make this ado, weeping and wailing?" He then states: "The girl (daughter of Jairus) is not dead but is sleeping." The reaction and response of the people toward Jesus: "They laughed Him to scorn (ridicule and derision)." When people lack faith and confidence in the power of God, they will always respond negatively and with doubts and derision. Jesus had Jairus clear these negative people out of the home. Those who remained were Jesus, Jairus, the girl's Mother, Peter, James and John. What will Jesus do next? Verses 41-43, Jesus took the 12-year old girl by the hand. He said to her, I say to you arise! Immediately, she arose. How did those in the home respond? How would the people who had scornfully rejected Jesus and His words react now? "They were ASTONISHED with a great ASTONISHMENT." Mark 5:42 (NLT) paraphrase is: "They were overwhelmed and totally amazed."

Another illustration where astonishment becomes central to the response of God's unique power being displayed is in Daniel 3. The chapter records that three men of faith and courage refused to bow down to the king's image. This infuriated King Nebuchadnezzar and he angrily directed that the three men be put to death in a furnace of fire. After the three men are thrown into the fiery furnace, the king sees four men walking about in the flames. What brought about this result? The three men of faith, courage and boldness had previously responded to the king: "Our God is able to deliver us...and He will deliver us...but even if He doesn't, we will not bow down to your image." When the king sees four men, Daniel 3:24 (ASV) records: "Then Nebuchadnezzar the king was ASTONISHED..." Other translations are: astounded (NASB); jumped up in alarm (Holman Bible); stood up in terror (International Standard Version); full of fear and wonder (Bible In Basic English); amazed (Modern KJV).

How do you respond to unexpected events which challenge one's imagination? It is basic that one must have faith and confidence in God's will. Situations may not always result in what "we want" but always and because of what "God wants" for our good and His glory.

Recently, a friend wrote about: How do we do Jesus? His suggested questions and answers:

Did Jesus rejoice with those who rejoice? He did at the wedding in Cana where he made the best wine ever.
Did Jesus mourn with those who mourn? Jesus wept!
Did Jesus live in harmony? He did with the woman at the well and His thanking her for giving Him water while reminding her about her many husbands – and she went and told everyone.
Did Jesus demonstrate, don't be proud? He did when He went to the home of Zacchaeus for lunch while the Pharisees were sure they were the ones who deserved lunch with Him.

It is alright for us to be astonished by His grace. In turn, we should be ready and willing to do astonishing things for Him. Astonishing grace will be the enabler for one to do astonishing and amazing things for Jesus Christ.

Recently, I was in a conversation with a young Pastor about ministry in general and about having the spirit and the will of never giving up. The conversation also included mentoring and whether or not he had Biblical heroes – those who stood head and shoulders above their contemporaries. After listening to my choices (Caleb in the OT; Epaphras and Barnabas in the NT), it seemed to me that he unhesitatingly replied: "My only hero is Jesus." That statement is true enough but misses a larger point that I was attempting to make. Why is Caleb a personal hero? It is because of the witness of Scripture (Numbers 32:11-12) that he followed the Lord wholeheartedly throughout his life. Epaphras (Colossians 4:12) is a personal hero because of the example he set as he labored in prayer for God's people that they would stand firm and be fully assured in all the will of God. Barnabas is a hero because of how he related to others. He knew how to embrace them as an encourager and instill hope and possibilities for them. At the time of Saul's conversion on the road to Damascus, Barnabas (Acts 9:27) would be available to encourage this new convert to his need for Jesus Christ to be his Lord rather than his adversary, and to gain his acceptance by the apostles. Any one of my personal heroes would share that one should never give up but always press on toward the goal and prize (Philippians 3:13-15).

In Our Daily Bread for Thursday - July 19, 2018 the following was shared:

My coworker Tom keeps an 8 X 12 glass cross on his desk. His friend Phil, who like Tom is a cancer survivor, gave it to him to help him look at everything through the cross. The glass cross is a constant reminder of God's love and good purposes for him. That's a challenging idea for all believers in Jesus, especially during difficult times...The apostle Paul's life was certainly an example of having a cross-shaped perspective. He described himself in times of suffering as being persecuted, but not abandoned; struck down, but not destroyed (Second Corinthians 4:9). He believed that in the hard times, God is at work, achieving for us an eternal glory that far outweighs them all. So we fix our eyes not on what is seen, but on what is unseen (vv. 17–18).

When Jesus was calling and training disciples, a scribe asked Jesus: "What is the greatest commandment of all?" Jesus replied that there is one standard set for God's people

and His chosen servants. In Mark 12:29-31, Jesus is quoting Deuteronomy 6:5 when he answered:
> *Hear O Israel, the Lord our God is One Lord, and you shall love the Lord your God with all your heart and with all your soul and with all your mind and with all your strength...Love your neighbor as yourself. No other commandment is greater than these.*

To love the Lord with "all your mind" can be challenging and daunting. I have personally and recently interacted with two of God's special people who have been facing the challenge of depression, despondency and moments of involuntary confusion. For those who have been receiving large amounts of medications for depression or cancer, there are moments when doubts, as well as lethargy and a sense of uselessness occur. During such times, certain and strange things come to the confused and despondent mind/brain (it is sometimes characterized as 'chemo-brain'). At all times, it serves one well to be reminded of Isaiah 41:9-10,
> *You are My servant. I have chosen and not rejected you. Do not fear, for I am with you; do not be afraid, for I am your God. I will strengthen you; I will surely help you; I will uphold you with My righteous right hand.*

Additionally, a contemporary worship chorus is helpful to review and pray. At the last church I served as Pastor, whenever song requests were being called for one young boy would always request the contemporary chorus based upon Psalm 119:105...
> *Thy Word is a lamp unto my feet*
> *and a light unto my path...*
> *When I feel afraid,*
> *Think I've lost my way,*
> *Still you're there right beside me.*

Becoming A Servant

*And nothing will I fear
As long as you are near.
Please be near me to the end....
I will not forget Your love for me and yet
My heart forever is wandering.
Jesus be my guide,
And hold me to your side,
I will love you to the end..."*

In a similar way, an older Hymn written by Fanny Crosby (1903) shares:

*Never be sad or desponding,
If thou hast faith to believe.
Grace, for the duties before thee,
Ask of thy God and receive.
Refrain:
Never give up, never give up,
Never give up to thy sorrows,
Jesus will bid them depart.
Trust in the Lord, trust in the Lord,
Sing when your trials are greatest,
Trust in the Lord and take heart.*

If you are downcast, discouraged, despondent or depressed r overwhelmed - don't give up. Look to Jesus Christ and be astonished by God's amazing grace in your behalf. Be grateful for His faithful care of you. You will be well served by reading and believing Galatians 6:8-9,

The one who sows to please the Spirit, from the Spirit will reap eternal life. Let us not grow weary in well-doing, for in due time we will reap a harvest, if we do not give up.

19. Powerful Grace

His divine power has given us everything we need for life and godliness through the knowledge of Him who called us by His own glory and excellence. Through these He has given us His precious and magnificent promises, so that through them you may become partakers of the divine nature, now that you have escaped the corruption in the world caused by evil desires.
Second Peter 1:3-4

    What does "divine power" mean for one's life and the choices one makes? What is the relationship one realizes through the "divine power" as it is linked to the "divine nature" and one's partaking of it? How do you understand divine power and its accessibility to the genuine Christian? What do these precious and magnificent assurances provide for a genuine Christian?
    In Biblical History, the times when failure seems to surface instead of victory is when one fails to make the wise choice of acting upon the divine power that is available. In First Kings 18, when Elijah gave the gathered people an opportunity to identify with the Living God rather than to Baal, he was met with silence. First Kings 18:21,
> *Elijah went before the people and said: How long will you waver between two opinions? If the Lord is God, follow him; but if Baal is God, follow him. But the people said nothing.*

    If divine power was sufficient to provide one with justification (the act of God's grace) and new life in Christ, why is it not utilized for life's everyday choices and decisions when the power and grace is always available to the followers of Jesus Christ. A factor to be considered entails one's readiness and willingness to make those major choices and decisions. These can be tipping points that separate victory from defeat; success from failure; pride from humility; commitment to a cause from mediocrity and matter-of-factness. Within the framework of servanthood and knowing the reality of powerful grace, obvious choices must be made. What is the basic decision a servant must make? How should all followers of Jesus Christ begin to be all of what the Master wants one to be? James 4:7-8 (NASB) responds:

> *Submit therefore to God. Resist the devil and he will flee from you. Draw near to God and He will draw near to you. Cleanse your hands, you sinners; and purify your hearts, you double-minded.*

According to James, what is the necessary decision of the servant of Jesus Christ? Clearly, it is: "Submit to God." The remaining acts – resisting, drawing near, cleansing and purifying – will all be fulfilled and become productive in one's complete submission.

In a similar way, Paul makes an impassioned appeal in Romans 12:1-2 where he beseeches (begs) the follower of Jesus Christ to desire the perfect will of God for one's life. He wrote:

> *I urge(beseech, beg) you…by the mercies of God, to present your bodies a living and holy sacrifice, acceptable to God, which is your spiritual service of worship. And do not be conformed to this world, but be transformed by the renewing of your mind, so that you may prove what the will of God is, that which is good and acceptable and perfect.*

According to Paul, what is the necessary decision of the servant of Jesus Christ? Clearly, it is: "Offering your bodies as a living sacrifice." What does this mean and what will it entail? One must be willing to sacrifice his/her personal agenda for God's greater purposes and an increased awareness of His powerful grace for one's life. This can involve radical behavioral change. It will affect one's natural instincts and innate negative actions or reactions. It is a measure of how genuine one is in terms of being a follower of Jesus Christ. It is more than merely saying "I believe" while being lethargic about and devoid of any purposeful and godly actions toward others. A devotional thought I read raised some practical questions about one's response to the needs of the moment and the requirements of God upon one's life. The questions raised and obvious response were:

> *What if Noah had told God: I don't do boats! What if Joseph had not forgiven his brothers and failed to protect them from the life-threatening famine? Or, what if Jesus had refused to die on the cross? Surrender is the tipping point. When we make that choice, God can use us to do great things for Him.*

The Hymn, *Take My Life, And Let It Be,* is often sung as one's consecration of life. When considering the priority of the will of God, the personal and relevant words of the hymn are:

> *Take my will, and make it Thine;*
> *It shall be no longer mine.*
> *Take my heart; it is Thine own;*
> *It shall be Thy royal throne.*

Joshua was called by God to lead His people into the Promised Land. The words and acts of Joshua emphasized that wise choices and clear distinctions had to be made when he challenged the people of his day to make an intelligent and logical spiritual choice. Without pause, he declared to all: "As for me and my household, we will serve the Lord" (Joshua 24:15). His Master was the Lord alone. The people of his day had vacillated between the cultural idols of that day and the idea that there was one true God who should be sought and obeyed. Their choices were often a matter of convenience rather than conviction. Joshua's words were clear cut and plain. Choose the idols of the day or the eternal God, the Creator of the universe. Their choice should've been immediate and decisive. Instead, they were hesitant and lacking decisiveness. How decisive have you been in your life as you have faced spiritual choices? Do you always opt for the way of the righteous or do you sometimes find attraction and comfort in some of the ways of the ungodly? The force of Joshua's words demonstrate the need for one to delve into his/her soul and determine who or what sits on the throne of one's heart. There is room for only one. The one to be seated on that throne should be – must be - Jesus Christ. You are His servant. One must respond affirmatively to: Is He your Savior, Lord and Master? The servant will then be seen in a different light. One's life will be lived in submission and obedience. One will model care for those who are lost and wandering in darkness. One will be a living sacrifice that desires only and always the perfect will of God for one's life. Powerful grace will exude from the servant who walks in the footsteps of Jesus. Such a one will consecrate his/her life daily. The focus and purpose will be to do the Master's agenda regardless of what it is or where it is.

    In 1936, J. Edwin Orr was at a Revival Meeting in New Zealand and was inspired to write the words to *Search Me, O God*. In one of the stanzas, he wrote: "O Holy Ghost, Revival comes from Thee; Send a revival, Start the work in me." He also penned the words that should be the song and prayer offered from and by the servant's heart and life:

> *Lord, take my life and make it wholly Thine;*
> *Fill my poor heart with Thy great love divine.*
> *Take all my will, my passion, self and pride;*
> *I now surrender,Lord—in me abide.*

20. A Living Legacy

Do we begin again to commend ourselves? Or do we need, as some others, epistles of commendation to you or letters of commendation from you? You are our epistle written in our hearts, known and read by all men; clearly you are an epistle of Christ, ministered by us, written not with ink but by the Spirit of the living God, not on tablets of stone but on tablets of flesh, that is, of the heart.
Second Corinthians 3:1-3

What is a legacy? There are three possibilities. First, it is a gift of personal property. Second, it is anything handed down from the past. Third, it is a specified and designated inheritance that is defined in a will. While this is the usual way to define and understand a legacy, the Apostle Paul indicates it can and should be something that is alive and vibrant. He makes this emphatic argument and statement in Second Corinthians 3:1-3 (MSG):

Does it sound like we're patting ourselves on the back, insisting on our credentials, asserting our authority? Well, we're not. Neither do we need letters of endorsement, either to you or from you. You yourselves are all the endorsement we need. Your very lives are a letter that anyone can read by just looking at you. Christ himself wrote it - not with ink, but with God's living Spirit; not chiseled into stone, but carved into human lives - and we publish it.

Our lives can and should represent a continuing legacy. It will include the difference we make now as well as the memories or that which one leaves behind. My wife and I have identified with many of David's comments in Psalm 37.

At the outset of our relationship together, Psalm 37:4,5 and 7(a) were significant and purposeful for us. The emphasis words – delight, trust, commit, rest, wait – all had and have significance in our lives. In later years, the words of Psalm 37:25-26 have been testified, prayed and claimed.

I have been young, and now am old, yet I have not seen the righteous forsaken or his children begging for bread. He is ever lending generously, and his children become a blessing.

These words have stimulated thoughts and questions that we can hopefully pass along to others. Questions such as: What is a purposeful life and legacy? How does one want his/her personage and life to be remembered by future generations? As one thinks about a legacy, a question about life was asked and answered in James 4:14. James wrote: "You do not know what tomorrow will bring. What is your life? For you are a mist that appears for a little time and then vanishes." The Psalmist had previously noted, Psalm 89:47, "Remember how fleeting is my life. For what futility you have created all humanity!" The NLT paraphrase is: "Remember how short my life is, how empty and futile this human existence! No one can live forever; all will die. No one can escape the power of the grave." The reality is that one's days have been numbered by the Lord. David observed in Psalm 139:16, "All my days were written in Your book and ordained for me before one of them came to be."

A larger question considers how one approaches life on each new day. No one knows what the events may be that enter one's life and decisions that will have to be made if/when they occur. We all have a schedule or routine planned but surprises can cause a shift in one's attention and action. In a common way, it is known as flexibility. Sometimes a person who is relatively insignificant and unknown can leave an important imprint on the lives of others. They may not even be aware of how their example is touching the lives of others.

In my first pastorate, there was a dear lady who set a good example for anyone who took notice. She had some physical limitations and her arthritis would flare up from time to time and limit her activity. If I mentioned her name, most people wouldn't know who she was or how her life would impact others. If one went by her home in the early morning hours, she would be found sitting on a rocker on her front porch. She would have her large, well-worn Bible opened on her lap. She would begin her day by praying the blessing that Moses had declared on the household of Asher, Deuteronomy 33:24-27. Her morning prayer was: "Lord, you have promised, as your days, so shall your strength be. You have kindly granted me another day and I need your strength for it." The Lord heard and honored her prayer and faithfulness. This dear lady left a legacy for others so they would also have confidence in the presence of God with them and His all-sufficient grace and strength for them (Isaiah 40:31, Second Corinthians 12:9).

Servanthood is not recognized by a title one may have or what a person may declare himself/herself to be. There was a man (Milton G.) who lived at a distance from the seaside community where we were living. He had a summer cabin near the ocean and would come to it on occasion. He was not known by many people but he is remembered by those who had the joy of meeting him and the giving spirit he exhibited. Milton would pay attention to various people and act kindly toward them. His life could be evaluated as one who went around doing good. My children can remember the different items he would drop off at our residence. He would do it without announcement or fanfare. We knew little about him and were never given his year-round resident address or telephone number. One Winter, due to unanticipated circumstances, the church we served was unable to pay our salary for seven weeks. We arrived at a time when we gathered our three little ones around the table and told them the food that was before them was our last meal. We also told them we were out of money and were unable to purchase any food. We all prayed that the Lord would look upon us with His mercy and meet our needs of the moment. I had to drive to a neighboring community to visit one who was ill. It was nighttime and the streets were very dark. On the main avenue through town, there were a couple of businesses that were open. A man stepped out from in front of his car and flagged me down. I thought he might have a special need or car trouble and I stopped. It was Milton G. He had come to the shore because of a plumbing problem in his home. He decided to shut down all the utilities and attend to the problem in the Spring. He indicated that he had cleared out their food cabinets and wondered if we could use any of the food items. He began to put the sacks into the back seat of my car and then asked me to wait while he went into the small grocery store. He brought out a case of 48 cans of Tuna Fish and hoped that it would be of help to us. When I returned home and had the children help me unload the bags, their eyes were open as wide as possible. Just an hour previously they had prayed for the Lord's provision and here was His immediate answer and provision. One of the prayer verses my wife and I have leaned on throughout the years is Isaiah 65:24, "It shall come to pass that before they call, I will answer; and while they are yet speaking, I will hear." The legacy of Milton G. is that he went about, unknown and unheralded, sensitive to the Lord's leading in his life, and doing immeasurable good. He will not be forgotten by those whose lives he touched and influenced.

  What is your legacy and how would you like to be remembered? A legacy is important because it is how one's life will be remembered. It's interesting to observe that Paul made the point of reminding Timothy of his heritage. In Second Timothy 1:3-8, he wrote the compelling words:

Becoming A Servant

I thank God, whom I serve with a pure conscience, as my forefathers did. Without ceasing, I remember you in my prayers night and day, greatly desiring to see you, being mindful of your tears, that I may be filled with joy, when I call to remembrance the genuine faith that is in you, which dwelt first in your grandmother Lois and your mother Eunice, and I am persuaded is in you also. Therefore, I remind you to stir up the gift of God which is in you through the laying on of my hands. For God has not given us a spirit of fear, but of power and of love and of a sound mind.

It was the legacy of genuine faith passed down to him from his Grandmother Lois and his Mother Eunice. His admonition is that Timothy not neglect or forget this precious legacy. Paul wants Timothy to stir up the gift of God and model the power of love and a sound mind.

A legacy is not just limited to older adults. There are times where a legacy can impact countless numbers of people by one who was very young and who struggled with debilitating maladies (children in Shriner's Hospitals or St. Jude's); a civil servant who impacted the lives of others by a courageous act in behalf of others; military personnel who performed heroic acts in combat; religious servants who made a significant difference in the lives of many people. While we could focus on many secular notables, I am drawn to spiritual people through several generations. Hebrews 11 is a type of roll call mentioning those who lived exceptional lives and accomplished great things in the name of the Lord. The criteria for entry into that chapter is summarized in verses 5-6: "By faith Enoch…was commended as one who pleased God. And without faith it is impossible to please God…"

When servant leaders were needed in the early church, Acts 6:3 indicates a basic requirement for the ones chosen to serve: "Select from among you seven men confirmed to be full of the Spirit and wisdom." Verse 5 indicates that one of the seven men selected was Stephen. "a man full of faith and of the Holy Spirit." Very quickly, verses 8-9 tell of Stephen being "…full of grace and power, was performing great wonders and signs among the people." As might be expected from the establishment religious groups "resistance arose." False charges were brought against him. In Acts 7:54-56 we find the religious community "…were enraged, and they gnashed their teeth at him." Stephen was undaunted by their opposition and was fearless. Verse 55-56 states:https://biblehub.com/acts/7-55.htm

> *Stephen, full of the Holy Spirit, looked intently into heaven and saw the glory of God and Jesus standing at the right hand of God. Look, he said, I see heaven open and the Son of Man standing at the right hand of God.*

This testimony of Stephen infuriated the opposition greatly and they dragged Stephen out of the city and began to stone him. His legacy is that he was a man of integrity, commitment, courage, and unafraid of any opposition to the message of the Lord.

Several people of the Scriptures could be selected as an example and with a legacy that could be emulated. Joshua and Caleb were men of faith and vision. They followed the Lord wholeheartedly all their lives. Daniel and his three friends were uncompromising. Their legacy was and is that they would not forsake the Lord God. Despite the threats of men and kings, they were bold in their witness and always carried out their opportunity to be a servant of the Lord. They did not fear death and were confident of the Lord's presence with them and as their deliverer from all trials they experienced.

There are many nameless, unknown, unheard of, insignificant people who have walked faithfully with the Lord and who did not fear any consequence that would come their way.

The commitment they made is consistent with the words of Paul in Philippians 1:20,

> *I eagerly expect and hope that I will in no way be ashamed, but will have complete boldness, so that now as always Christ will be exalted in my body, whether by life or by death.*

This is the legacy of many, unnamed and unknown, who learned the lessons and values of servanthood. It caused them to follow the Master unswervingly and faithfully.

What is your legacy? Regardless of your age, is your walk of faith exemplary? Do you model what it is to live in the presence of Jesus Christ? Be encouraged to order your life in accord with the words of the Psalmist:

> *The Lord directs the steps of the godly.*
> *He delights in every detail of their lives.*
> *Though they stumble, they will never fall,*
> *for the Lord holds them by the hand.*
> *Once I was young, and now I am old.*
> *Yet I have never seen the godly abandoned*
> *or their children begging for bread.*
> *The godly always give generous loans to others,*
> *and their children are a blessing.*
> *Psalm 37:23-26*

21. Loneliness

Sing to God! Sing praises to His name. Exalt the One who rides on the clouds, His name is the Lord and rejoice before Him. A father of the fatherless, and a defender of the widows, is God in His holy habitation. God settles the lonely in families; He leads the prisoners out to prosperity...
Psalm 68:4-6

    The Bible begins with the story of the six days of creation by Almighty God. In the summary of creation, one can gain an insight into the mind of God about His perfect and very good creation, especially as it pertains to man in Genesis 2:18,"The Lord God said: It is not good for the man to be alone. I will make a helper suitable for him." At the outset of creation, there is a concern about the possibility and potential of aloneness (loneliness). God provides a helper for Man and in doing so establishes the purpose and groundwork for marriage. Genesis 2:24 states: "That is why a man leaves his father and mother and is united to his wife, and they become one flesh." The Apostle Paul echoes these precise words when he emphasizes what constitutes marriage in the sight of God (Ephesians 5:21-33). In verse 31, Paul wrote (echoed): "That is why a man leaves his father and mother and is united to his wife, and they become one flesh." Among the many reasons for marriage, one of the primary purposes is to prevent a man's loneliness.

    Loneliness is defined as sadness because one has no friends or company. It is not only marked by sadness, it can also move one toward introversion and depression. There is a comical and important insight into loneliness when Charles Schulz, who was very creative with the characters in his Peanuts comic strip, gave an account of Charlie Brown and

Lucy's Psychiatry booth. The story line is: Charlie Brown visited Lucy's psychiatry booth and asked her a simple question: "Can you cure loneliness?" Her response was trite. She said: "For a nickel, I can cure anything." Charlie Brown delved into her abilities by asking: "Can you cure deep-down, black, bottom-of-the-well, no-hope, end-of-the-world, what's-the-use loneliness?" How would the "psychiatrist" Lucy respond to such an all-encompassing inquiry. True to character and unemotionally, she barked: "For the same nickel?!"

Psychology Today, April 2018, produced a report from their Loneliness Research Study. In that report, they indicated that loneliness can cause considerable pain in one's brain and body. They indicated that the feeling of loneliness can be overwhelming as one deals with their sense of rejection and disconnection. The fact is that loneliness is no respecter of persons. It can be a reality for the very young through all age brackets. It doesn't matter where one lives or if they are married or single. The sense and feeling of aloneness can overwhelm one – anyone – at any time. It has been generally suggested that loneliness is a malady that hides in plain sight. It is often not seen or discerned and is easily overlooked or minimized even by one's close associates. For the one enduring aloneness and feeling the pain of loneliness, every day is like another building block that allows the inner void to become larger and larger - greater and greater.

The Psychology Today research indicated the serious physical downside to loneliness. They indicated that lonely people are more likely than non-lonely people to die from cardiovascular disease, cancer, respiratory illness and other lesser maladies. It is crucial to determine how widespread the condition of loneliness has extended. Sometimes it can be detected because of a behavioral shift by an individual. There is a type of aura from the despondent, discouraged, depressed and lonely person. The perceptive and discerning person needs to have this awareness about those with whom there is relatively close association. Why? Because the studies have indicated loneliness does not always equate with one being alone. It is determined by how a person feels inwardly. One may have several friends but still feel isolated and alone.

One way of being sensitive to where another person is emotionally requires one's awareness that feelings of chronic loneliness can be hurtful and harmful for an individual. One area for concern is an increasing indication of cognitive decline and the onset of dementia. Psychology Today concluded in its study that "lonely people are more than twice as likely to develop Alzheimer's as the non-lonely."

Is it possible for a follower of Christ, a servant, to be lonely? In 2011, Billy Graham wrote a paper on the subject of loneliness. It was titled: *Are You Lonely?* Part of what he wrote included:

> *One day I went for a walk to meditate. As I watched a bird sitting alone on a fencepost, I thought about a passage of Scripture found in the 102nd Psalm: I am like a pelican of the wilderness: I am like an owl of the desert. I lie awake, and am like a sparrow alone on the housetop (Psalm 102:6-7). Are you lonely? There are many lonely people today. Loneliness is one of the supreme problems of modern society. Loneliness has an inner dimension. It is a thirst of the spirit, and the roots of loneliness are within each of us...It was never God's intention for you to be lonely.*

I have friends and acquaintances who have privately shared that they feel "used" and are "unappreciated." They serve faithfully and well - even better than some who are in the spotlight and are recipients of accolades. Is it right for that to occur? No! Does it happen within your circle of friends? Yes! Is there anything you can do about it? The answer should be a resounding "Yes"! There is always something that can be done. From a negative viewpoint, some would suggest it is doubtful. From the positive mindset, the response is that it may take time for it to take place but you can and should make a difference in the lives of others.

Some have retired from ministry and now feel alone, isolated and/or ignored. A Pastor's wife echoed some thoughts from her heart after reading a published article posted on August 10, 2018 by Shari Thomas: *10 Things the Woman Married to Your Pastor Wants You to Know*. Now that her husband has retired after many years of devoted and energetic ministry, she wrote: "This truth has been the most devastating. Many women discover, when their husband leaves a pastoral position, that people they thought were friends really weren't. They assumed the Christmas cards, social invites, long conversations over coffee, or trips to the beach were due to friendships. It's devastating to discover that, without his role, the friendship was never really there." My feeble effort of a response stated:

> *Well said - and - thank you for saying it. People in the pew have no idea of the 'loneliness' that occurs when 'friends' seem to avoid and/or ignore those who invested their personal lives and family into the lives of the congregants... It's like being thrown to the curb (treated as something of no value) or thrown under the bus (as though you no longer exist, or are no longer needed)... If it wasn't for Jesus, how lonely life would be....*

Later, after reading the published article and giving further thought and prayer to what was shared, I added a larger response:

> *I have a friendship with a very gifted retired Seminary Professor. He is an excellent speaker and has spoken before large assemblies and classes, - BUT - he's gone more than 4 years without being invited anywhere to speak. He is a man whose life was devoted to his students. They consumed his private life as well desiring*

Becoming A Servant

to be with him and to learn from him. NOW - no one seems to remember him or his wife. A sad chapter in the life of one who still has much to share. I was bemoaning with him that so few people respond to the Blogs I write and post. By way of "encouragement", he wrote me that of his last 192 posts, he's had only 2 respondents... That is sad and painful for this man - a wise, factual and brilliant writer. I think he should publish his work product - hopefully - he will.
When I graduated from Grammar School, we were awarded a bronze lapel pin on which were the inscribed words: Nil Desperandum(Never Despair).

In my personal moments of being in the doldrums (which don't last very long) or feeling the effects of aloneness, I make myself ask a question - Who are you serving - people or Jesus Christ? When this question is answered correctly, there is the awareness of the Lord's powerful grace upholding me and the sense that ultimately He will honor those who honor Him (First Samuel 2:30; Second Timothy 2:11-13). I was also helped and encouraged by the Devotion, *Insight For Living* by Charles R. Swindoll on Friday; August 10th, 2018:

Do I write to you who serve behind the scenes in a ministry or a business? You work faithfully and diligently, yet the glory goes to another. Your efforts make someone else successful. How easy to feel resentful...take heart! Our God who rewards in secret will never overlook your commitment. 'For God is not unjust so as to forget your work and the love which you have shown toward His name, in having ministered and in still ministering to the saints' (Hebrews 6:10). A great verse for those of you who feel used and unappreciated. Do you serve behind the scenes? Take heart! Our God who rewards in secret won't overlook your commitment.

James Perry

Robert Harkness (1880-1961) was an Australian songwriter. He explained how he had come to write the hymn: *No Longer Lonely.*

He spoke about the sad battle at Gallipoli. It was only a few years after the end of the war (1916) and the end of the Gallipoli landing by the Anzacs and other expeditionary corps. He was part of the preaching team on tour in the outback of Australia with an evangelist. Following the evening meeting they were taken to a wealthy sheep station owner for overnight lodging. In the spacious living room was a beautiful piano. He walked over to it, thinking he would play a few hymns before they all retired. Abruptly, the lady of the house prevented him, You cannot play this piano! Why not? he asked in shock. The lady went on to explain the sad story behind it. My son was a student in the medical school of the university. He was also very good on the piano. He used to sit and play for hours at a time. The house was filled with music. Then one day, he was drafted and was sent to Gallipoli with the Anzacs, never to return. I can't bear the thought of anyone playing our son's piano. His memory is unforgettable and extremely painful for me. Mr. Harkness...opening his New Testament and read from First Peter 5:7, 'Cast all your anxieties on him, for he cares about you.' The next morning the lady cheerfully called them for breakfast and greeted them with, 'I'm no longer lonely...Jesus is the Friend of friends to me.' A note was struck in Mr. Harkness' heart; may I put it to music? Oh, please do, she said. On the piano which had been a dead monument, it came alive with the strains of No Longer Lonely. The words and music flowed from his pen onto the keys of the neglected piano, expressing the joy and hope of having Jesus as "the Friend of friends to me.

On life's pathway I am never lonely,
My Lord is with me, my Lord divine;
Ever present guide, I trust Him only,
No longer lonely, for He is mine.

I shall not be lonely in my sorrow,
He will sustain me until the end;
Darkest night He turns to brightest morrow,
No longer lonely! He is my friend.

I shall not be lonely in the valley
Though' shadows gather, I will not fear;
He has promised ever to uphold me,
No longer lonely! He will be near.
Refrain:
No longer lonely, no longer lonely,
For Jesus is the friend of friends to me;
No longer lonely, no longer lonely,
For Jesus is the friend of friends to me.
(Cyber Hymnal – Public Domain)

I had been thinking about the impact when one has a "Being Downcast" moment - the feelings of sadness, negativity about life, loneliness, being lethargic, despairing – searching for something – but having a sense of emptiness, aloneness or uselessness. In some cases, there is no sound reason for the way a person is feeling or being observed. In other instances, there is a possible explanation. Being downcast can come upon a person when there is no advanced warning or indication of what is internally taking place and for which one can be prepared. When one is in chemotherapy, things can occur emotionally and mentally for which one can be ill-prepared such as "chemo-brain". One of the interesting things about chemo-brain is that one's peers or close friends do not always understand what is causing particular reactions and responses – and – don't really know what to say. I have a friend who has the uncanny ability to write a note or make a call that lifts my spirit when I feel helpless, useless, unworthy, and no future place for ministry. Early this morning a dear man of God whom I have promised to uphold in prayer and whom I was thinking of shared that he was "feeling down." I shared with this brother in Christ a personal note I had recently received. It stated: "I enjoy and learn from your posts. Thank you! Thank you for all you have done for me and your friendship through the years. God bless you and yours!" I don't know how such a note would impact you, but it caused my spirit to soar. For my downcast friend(s), I wrote: "Keep on looking to Jesus" (Hebrews 12:2). For my negative acquaintances and friends, "Trust in the Lord with all your heart, and lean not to your own understanding" (Proverbs 3:5). For my insensitive peers and discouraged colleagues – especially those who feel squeezed out of ministry, be reminded of God's Word: "Open your mouth wide, and I will fill it" (Psalm 81:10). And – to the reluctant servant Moses, the Lord heard and replied:

- What if they won't believe me or listen to me?
- What if they say: The Lord never appeared to you?

Then the Lord asked him, What is that in your hand? A shepherd's staff, Moses replied. Just a staff that would be used by the Lord to guide His people to their promised land (Exodus 4).

I was also reading two Psalms (42 and 43) where the Psalmist's question about being downcast is raised and answered: (42:5) "Why are you downcast, O my soul? Why the unease within me? Put your hope in God, for I shall yet praise Him for the salvation of His presence." The same question and answer is given in the following Psalm (43:5), "Why are you downcast, O my soul? Why the unease within

Becoming A Servant

me? Put your hope in God, for I shall yet praise Him, my Savior and my God." It is good and wise counsel, but not always easy to do when one feels overwhelmed on the one hand, and no longer useful or needed on the other. When this has happened with me, I am so thankful for a godly wife who gently says: "C'mon, Jimmy, you are going to be alright and God is still using you. I am so proud of you..." Wow! Just writing it brings tears to my eyes.

There is a well-known Hymn that should be remembered and often referenced. It includes the following thoughts of hope and encouragement:

Why should I feel discouraged,
why should the shadows come,
Why should my heart be lonely,
and long for heaven and home,
When Jesus is my portion?
My constant friend is He:
His eye is on the sparrow,
and I know He watches me.

Refrain:

I sing because I'm happy,
I sing because I'm free,
For His eye is on the sparrow,
And I know He watches me.

Everyone has moments when they have a sense of loneliness. What can you do to alleviate that sense in others? What can you do to alleviate it in yourself? If you contacted a friend, family member or a person who lives alone – that could serve a dual purpose. It would be an encouragement for another individual – and – it can cause you to forget about your own sense of loneliness or unworthiness. Try it – you may find out that you like it and have been benefitted by touching another's life.

James Perry

In March 2013, *Sojourners Magazine* printed an article about *A Cup of Cold Water*. A summation comment was:
> *A cup of cold water is the minimal requirement for what the Scripture calls hospitality or in the original language, xenophilia - love of the stranger. Jesus says that whoever gives a cup of cold water to these nomadic disciples will not fail to receive their reward. Hospitality is a Christian virtue. The writer of the book of Hebrews reminds us, "Do not forget to show hospitality to strangers for some have entertained angels unaware" (Hebrews 13:2).*

For the weary, lonely, disenfranchised, homeless person, a display of care and friendship will encourage the discouraged; replace a smile for a frown; give a sense of worth for those who have felt unworthy. You can and should do this in Jesus name and for one of the least of these who go unnoticed. Will you make a difference in the life of one who is lonely? May the Lord bless and use you as you bring glory to His name.

22. Being Alone

Since you were precious in My sight, You have been honored, And I have loved you...Fear not, for I am with you.
Isaiah 43:4-5 (NKJV)

Don't be obsessed with getting more material things. Be relaxed with what you have. Since God assured us, "I'll never let you down, never walk off and leave you," we can boldly quote, God is there, ready to help; I'm fearless no matter what. Who or what can get to me?
Hebrews 13:5-6 (MSG)

A statement attributed to Orson Welles gives a fatalistic view of a person's life. "We're born alone, we live alone, we die alone. Only through our love and friendship can we create the illusion for the moment that we're not alone." By contrast, a statement listed in Good Quotes states: "True friendship isn't about being inseparable, it's about being separated and knowing nothing will change." Against the backdrop of these two statements are the commissioning words of Moses to Joshua as he prepared to lead the people of God into The Promised Land (Deuteronomy 31:7-8):

> *Be strong and courageous, for you will go with this people into the land the Lord swore to their fathers to give them, and you shall give it to them as an inheritance. The Lord Himself goes before you; He will be with you. He will never leave you or forsake you. Do not be afraid or discouraged.*

These words will be repeated and recorded in Joshua 1:6-9 to remind him of his commission and God's expectation for his life:

Be strong and of good courage, for to this people you shall divide as an inheritance the land which I swore to their fathers to give them. Only be strong and very courageous, that you may observe to do according to all the law which Moses My servant commanded you; do not turn from it to the right hand or to the left, that you may prosper wherever you go. This Book of the Law shall not depart from your mouth, but you shall meditate in it day and night, that you may observe to do according to all that is written in it. For then you will make your way prosperous, and then you will have good success. Have I not commanded you? Be strong and of good courage; do not be afraid, nor be dismayed, for the Lord your God is with you wherever you go.

    Joshua and Caleb were used to having to stand alone and to follow the Lord wholeheartedly. They are finally arriving at the earthly home the Lord had apportioned for His people. Joshua will have to lead them and Caleb will have to assist them in order for God's people to possess the land of promise. You and I have the same privilege of being strong and courageous for the Lord even when it requires us to stand and be alone. The Lord wants us to always remember that His grace and ability is always more than sufficient for the challenges and opportunities we face. There will always be some naysayers who would rather be left alone and be alone than to apply and exert themselves to achieve God's goals for them. Being alone sounds more ideal than it actually is. It can have moments of peace, relief and freedom, but it soon pales when there is no one present for conversation or communication of any sort and peace in one's heart and life is absent.

    In part, being alone is illustrated by a film from 1990, *Home Alone*. The plot of the story is:

Becoming A Servant

Kevin McCallister, is mistakenly left behind when his family flies to Paris for their Christmas vacation. Kevin, had been ridiculed by his siblings and cousins. A fight with his older brother, Buzz, resulted in Kevin getting sent to the third floor of the house for punishment, where he wished that his family would disappear. During the night, heavy winds cause damage to power lines, which causes a temporary power outage and resets the alarm clocks, causing the entire family to oversleep. In the confusion and rush to get to the airport, Kevin is accidentally left behind. He awakens to find the house empty and, thinking his wish has come true, is overjoyed with his newfound freedom.

While Kevin initially relished being alone and having the house all to himself, he soon begins to feel the pangs of loneliness and having to deal with fears of the unknown. One of his fears is the next-door neighbor, Old Man Marley, who had been rumored to have murdered his family with a snow shovel. With people being away for the holiday, burglars roam the neighborhood looking for places where they can gain easy access. Kevin will have to cope with the bungling burglars, Harry and Marv. He does so with a series of tricks he concocts, along with obstacles he devised. However, Kevin's time of adventure and freedom comes to a moment of reality. He misses his family and finds that being alone is not all of what he had thought and hoped it would be.

In a micro-cosmic way, this is a truism for anyone who would like to escape the realities of life. The Alcoholic attempts to do it with beverages and the gradual escalation of imbibing those with greater alcoholic content. The Drug Addict attempts to dull his sense of reality by graduating from a lesser mood modifier, Marijuana (a psychoactive drug), into the habit-forming drugs such as heroin, cocaine, meth amphetamines, opioids, etc. Much of this is a means to escape stress, tension, depression and realities of life in general.

In a devotional posted by Joseph Stowell, August 11, 2018, *Supremely Significant* we read that:

> *Modern counseling and psychology focus a lot of attention on obsessive behaviors, whether it's an obsession with food, tobacco, alcohol, pornography, drugs, or even work. But perhaps one of the most overlooked addictions is our obsession with personal significance. Think about the amount of time and energy you spend in maintaining, advancing, expanding, and protecting your sense of significance. You know, making yourself look good, staying on top of the heap, protecting your ego, and living to be more successful than the next guy.*

In actuality, without knowing it, such a one will arrive at the place of significance that was sought and realize they are alone at the top. Can this drive for significance be part of the goal and motivation of a servant of God? Will such a one disregard the abilities and feelings of another to gain the position or prestige one hopes to gain? Should the one who has been used, unappreciated, disregarded, ignored by the ambitious and self-indulgent person seek to assert his own will and rights in order to gain some level of significance? The answer should be a resounding "No!" Joseph Stowell continued his devotional with the following:

> *Significance is often gained at the expense of our character as we are willing to lie and cut ethical corners to be viewed well by others. It makes us defensive when someone seeks to improve us through criticism. The pursuit embitters our hearts against God over disappointing and unchangeable personal issues like our size, shape, or color. Pursuing our own significance makes us vulnerable to a host of verbal sins, such as gossip, slander, boasting, lying, and immoral chatter.*

Becoming A Servant

Personal ambition can often miss the bigger picture. One cannot know what events will come along and favor the one who has been systematically passed by. We would be remiss if we failed to note Genesis 37 through 50 and the character issues that were important to Joseph. The range of events that occurred in the life of Joseph include the hatred of his brothers; their desire to kill him but opt for selling him to some slave owners; his being in Egypt (alone, separated from his father and family); His being imprisoned; betrayed by the Baker and Candlestick Maker he had aided and befriended; the attempt of Potiphar's wife to entice him into an immoral relationship; and having to stand alone while being alone for the values of Almighty God.

During a time of great need in the nation and that part of the world, because of the vision and skill of Joseph, Egypt found itself as the central power and means for the world's survival. When Jacob sends his sons for grain and food, Joseph recognizes them and has the power to do whatever he pleased by way of retaliation. Would he have them arrested and punished? Would he send them away with empty sacks and allow them to perish? How will the brothers respond to Joseph? How will he respond to their fictional and deceitful ways?

In Genesis 50:15-17, the brothers falsify what their father Jacob had said. They are looking to preserve their lives and connive among themselves of how best they can achieve their self-indulgence. They are thinking that Joseph would reciprocate and do to them that which they had wanted to do to him. They fail to think of the character traits each of them should've had all along. They do not know Joseph and how he was God's man for such a time as this. The brothers resort to falling down before him (verse 18) and declaring: "Behold, we are your servants." How would you have responded to these men and their wicked scheming? Would you have used this moment to retaliate and let them feel the pain and anguish of being alone and at the mercy of others? How do you act and react in the alone and away places of your life? Do you represent Jesus only or someone/something else?

Joseph responded with mercy, compassion and grace. Genesis 50:19-21 records Joseph's words and actions:

Do not be afraid, for am I in the place of God? But as for you, you meant evil against me; but God meant it for good, in order to bring it about as it is this day, to save many people alive. Now therefore, do not be afraid; I will provide for you and your little ones. And he comforted them and spoke kindly to them.

If only each of us would have the character and attitude of Joseph. He submitted to God and His will for his life. He represented to the fearful that there was hope in the Lord. He behaved toward those who wanted to harm him with tenderness, compassion, comfort and forgiveness. It caused me to reflect on some of the concluding words of Joseph Stowell in his devotional:

I need to add, being driven to protect and advance our sense of significance renders us unable to serve others unless there is an advantage to be gained; unable to sacrifice for a cause that is not our own and unwilling to suffer for that cause if necessary; unable to surrender to any agenda that impedes the progress of our personal persona. In short, it cripples our ability to love God more than ourselves and to live to bring glory to God since, when we are compelled to glorify ourselves, we are unable to exalt His worthy significance.

The body of Jesus Christ, His Church, and all who are His followers/servants are supposed to be channels of the love, mercy, grace, compassion and comfort of our Master. Jesus

Becoming A Servant

describes what being a channel for Him will entail, Matthew 10:16-20 (NKJV),

> *I send you out as sheep in the midst of wolves. Be wise as serpents and harmless as doves. But beware of men, for they will deliver you up to councils and scourge you in their synagogues. You will be brought before governors and kings for My sake, as a testimony to them and to the Gentiles. But when they deliver you up, do not worry about how or what you should speak. For it will be given to you in that hour what you should speak; for it is not you who speak, but the Spirit of your Father who speaks in you (and through you).*

The Lord is seeking dependable laborers who will faithfully serve Him today. The United Methodist Hymnal (1989) included a Hymn that became an immediate favorite. The hope is that the words will be resuscitated in the lives of those who follow Jesus Christ. *Here I Am, Lord*, written by Dan Schutte. The first stanza asks and the Refrain responds:

> *Who will bear my light to them?*
> *Whom shall I send?*

The Refrain:

> *Here I am, Lord. Is it I Lord?*
> *I have heard you calling in the night.*
> *I will go, Lord, if you lead me.*

23. Hearing and Heeding

But you do not believe, because you are not of My sheep, as I said to you. My sheep hear My voice, and I know them, and they follow Me. And I give them eternal life, and they shall never perish; neither shall anyone snatch them out of My hand.
John 10:26-28 (NKJV)

    Jesus began His earthly ministry by selecting men who became His disciples (Matthew 4:18-22). His call to them was precise and clear, "Follow Me." Without hesitancy or reluctance, their response was: "They immediately followed Him." Jesus Christ will go on to describe Himself as the, "I Am." This went beyond the analogous description He gave, such as being the light; the bread of life; the resurrection and life; the way truth and life; etc. He is, in fact declaring that He is Jehovah in the midst of a people He is calling and shaping to be His followers.
    By using the "I am" identifier, Jesus indicates that the response of God to Moses' inquiry in Exodus 3:11-14 about the authority by which Moses is called to lead a people out of bondage is "I Am Who I Am" is in control of Pharaoh and the events that will follow. Jesus is informing His disciples and other followers, the "I Am" in Exodus 3 is the "I Am" who is present them.
    Just as Moses was expected to respond affirmatively to the direction of "I AM", the disciples are also expected to respond to "I AM" who is with them and has called them to follow Him. This same message is conveyed to all who will affirm their faith in Jesus Christ. Jesus refers to those who respond as being His sheep who have heard His voice and are following Him (John 10:27). The idea of sheep who follow a

shepherd is not just a Gospel concept. This truth was understood and embraced by David as recorded in Psalm 23. He had come to know and appreciate the uniqueness of a shepherd who cares for and leads a flock. From the lessons he had learned as a young shepherd, he would write and sing Psalm 23. The words were reassuring to him as he confronted responsibilities and dangers.

When the Philistine army gathered to enter combat with Israel, they had the champion Goliath who would come into the valley and roar out his words of derision and intimidation. King Saul and his army were filled with fear and knew they were unequal to the task of defending themselves. But then, the youngest son of Jesse was sent to bring food to his brothers and others and also to assess the war situation and report back to his father. Ultimately, David will volunteer to face Goliath. King Saul doesn't believe the fate of the nation should rest with a boy combatting a giant. However, David gives a type of Job Description that he believes qualifies him for the task. He relates some of his experiences as a shepherd who cares for and protects his sheep. David said to King Saul, I Samuel 17:34-37,

> *Your servant used to keep his father's sheep, and when a lion or a bear came and took a lamb out of the flock, I went out after it and struck it, and delivered the lamb from its mouth; and when it arose against me, I caught it by its beard, and struck and killed it. Your servant has killed both lion and bear; and this uncircumcised Philistine will be like one of them, seeing he has defied the armies of the living God. Moreover, David said: The Lord, who delivered me from the paw of the lion and from the paw of the bear, He will deliver me from the hand of this Philistine.*

One of David's brothers, Eliab, is critical, annoyed and disparaging. His indignation boils over because of David volunteering that he alone could conquer a giant, while the army of Israel cringed in fear as Goliath taunted them. I Samuel 17:28, records Eliab's indignation:

> *Now Eliab his oldest brother heard when he spoke to the men; and Eliab's anger was aroused against David, and he said: Why did you come down here? And with whom have you left those few sheep in the wilderness? I know your pride and the insolence of your heart, for you have come down to see the battle.*

It was very obvious that most of the people were in agreement with Eliab rather than with David. Even though he was young, David was by no means naïve. His response to Eliab and others is wistful but also thought-provoking. David responded, I Samuel 17:29-30,

> *What have I done now? Is there not a cause? Then he turned from him toward another and said the same thing; and these people answered him as the first ones did.*

In other words, David's confidence was at variance with the people of Israel. Their entire future was going to rest with this young man whose only weapon was a slingshot. The brothers and others needed to think through the possibilities of David's questions: "What have I done now?" and, "Is there not a cause?" What David is about to do by the will and direction of "I AM" will answer those questions. "I AM" will use him to conquer a giant and defeat an enemy. Just a boy with a slingshot and five stones against a giant in full armor and weaponry.

David not only had to listen to the angry words of his brothers and others, he would also have to listen to the words of derision uttered by Goliath and deal with his attitude, (verses 42-44),

> *(Goliath) disdained him; for he was only a youth, ruddy and good-looking. So Goliath said to David: Am I a dog, that you come to me with sticks? And the Philistine cursed David by his gods. And the Philistine said to David: Come to me, and I will give your flesh to the birds of the air and the beasts of the field!*

One can only imagine how thunderous those words sounded as they echoed through the valley. What was David thinking? What was his strategy? Was he afraid? If not, why not? Anyone in his right mind would feel overwhelmed by such words and confrontation. Could it be that the words coursing through the heart and mind of David were the words that would be included in Psalm 23? Think of the phrases: "The Lord is MY Shepherd...HE leads me...even though I walk through the valley of the shadow of death...I will fear no evil...MY Shepherd is with me...HE will prepare a table for be before the presence of my enemies..." David's response to Goliath, Verses 45-47, bears out those words of trust, faith, confidence and assurance.

> *You come to me with a sword, with a spear, and with a javelin. But I come to you in the name of the Lord of hosts, the God of the armies of Israel, whom you have defied. This day the Lord will deliver you into my hand, and I will strike you and take your head from you. And this day I will give the carcasses of the camp of the Philistines to the birds of the air and the wild beasts of the earth, that all the earth may know that there is a God in Israel. Then all this assembly shall know that the Lord does not save with sword and spear; for the battle is the Lord's, and He will give you into our hands.*

Becoming A Servant

Take special note of the last phrase spoken by David, "The Lord will give you into OUR hands." David is indicating that despite all the anger, doubts and second-guessing whether or not David should represent Israel against the Philistines, David never wavered about his role and task of the moment. He was not racing toward Goliath with any desire for personal aggrandizement, but was vicariously confronting the giant for all of the people and nation. A shepherd boy unafraid of the dangerous encounter. A shepherd boy who had conquered his fears because of the hand of God upon his life.

This is the lesson Jesus wanted His disciples to learn and do. They are to be confident that "I AM" has called them to accomplish an assigned task. In the process of their learning the lessons being taught and demonstrated by Jesus, there is an important purpose He wants them to learn and in which they are to trust. He shares that truth in John 13:15-17 (NKJV) as he observes the Passover with them. Jesus has assumed the role of a servant and washed their feet. He then says to them:

> *For I have given you an example, that you should do as I have done to you. Most assuredly, I say to you, a servant is not greater than his master; nor is he who is sent greater than he who sent him. If you know these things, blessed are you if you do them.*

The phrase that the disciples and we are to hear and heed are: "If you know these things, blessed are you if you do them." It is a reminder that servanthood is much more than what one may think or say. The servant-disciple is measured by what one is becoming and doing – "Blessed are you if you do them." A pedagogical principle impacts one's students in terms of what they are to know, think and do. Good Pedagogy also includes additional objectives that will impact the areas of motivation, exposition, direction of activity, criticism and inviting imitation (modeling). While this is the secular objective, it is also a lesson which Jesus taught in John 13, "I have given you an example" and "if you know these things…do them." Was this optional? No! Jesus expected His disciples and followers to follow His example and to do the things He modelled for them.

Hymns of consecration can be useful as a prayer for one's life. One hymn that should resonate was written in 1905 by W. H. Pike,

O gracious God, on Thee I wait,
With Thine own self my being fill;
As day by day my life I live,
To do Thy will, Thy blessed will.

Refrain:
To do Thy will, yes, that is all;
To do Thy will, obey Thy call;
To follow, Lord, where Thou dost lead,
To do Thy will is all I need.

24. Honored

Render therefore to all their due: taxes to whom taxes are due, customs to whom customs, fear to whom fear, honor to whom honor…
                             Romans 13:7-8 (NKJV)

Since you were precious in My sight, You have been honored,..
                             Isaiah 43:4-5

The Lord declares…Those who honor me I will honor…
                             First Samuel 2:30

      Honor, when used as a noun means: "a source of credit or distinction; high respect." When used as a verb, it means: "to show a courteous regard for one." Honor in our society is rendered in different ways. When a military person has performed exceptionally and excellently, above and beyond the call of duty, such a one receives the highest award possible by a grateful nation, The Congressional Medal of Honor. A civilian who has done the same receives The Presidential Medal of Freedom.
      One of the usages of the word honor is to view someone with high respect. This would include honoring God by one's worship and commitment. Honoring includes the necessity to render respect to one's parents. As a parent ages, he/she may dress, speak or behave in ways that are different than the norm and might become an embarrassment to his/her children. What should the child/children do when instances of feeble-mindedness or dementia begins to be evident? The Biblical requirement is to exercise a love that covers over the things that may be embarrassing or cause family uneasiness. First Peter 4:8 states the general guideline that should be

followed in all relationships: "Above all, love one another deeply, because love covers over a multitude of sins."

When Peter wrote that love covers over a multitude of sins, what motivated him to write these words? What personal background did he have that evoked this act of kindness and consideration toward another? It is interesting to note that the translation of the word "cover" infers and could just as easily be translated "forgive." It appears that he learned this principle from Jesus Christ (Matthew 18:21-22) when he asked Jesus: "How often shall I forgive my brother who sins against me?" Peter adds a limitation qualifier: "Up to seven times?" We do not know with certainty why Peter would pose the question as he did. The primary point to be understood and lesson to be implemented is the answer given to him by Jesus Christ: "I do not say to you up to seven times, but up to seventy times seven." It defines further that which Paul wrote in First Corinthians 13:5, "Love keeps no record of wrongs." In the Amplified NT, it is expressed: "Love doesn't keep score of the sins of others."

There is also the guideline in First Corinthians 13:4, "Love is patient, love is kind." When these guidelines are applied toward one's parent(s), how does one show a love that covers over a parental foible, frailty or unconventional behavior? Should the child confront the parent in harsh terms or actions, or with patience and kindness? Should there be confrontation and pointing out negatives felt toward a parent? What is the best way to honor a parent – even in their aging years? Grimm's Fairy Tales include this story:

> *Once there was an old man whose eyes blinked continually, and whose hands trembled uncontrollably. As he had no place to live, he moved in with his son's family. His daughter-in-law hated it when at the dinner table he constantly rattled his silverware and spilled his drinks. In anger and exasperation she insisted he eat his meals alone in the corner, separated from the rest*

of the family. He began to eat alone, looking occasionally at the family sitting at the table. Then, one day, when his hands were shaking so much that he knocked his bowl onto the floor, his meal spilt onto the carpet. The daughter-in-law screamed: If you are going to eat like a pig we'll feed you like a pig! She placed a wooden trough on the floor and told him that he would have to eat out of the trough like an animal. This he did.

Some days later the woman's young son came into the house excited to show her something he had made: Look Mommy! I've made a trough to feed you and Daddy out of when I get big.

The woman began to cry as she realized what a terrible evil she was guilty of. From that day forward the old man ate his meals at the table with the rest of the family and the daughter-in-law did everything she could to make up for the cruel way that she had treated her father-in-law.

The word of God speaks of the aged in very kind and descriptive ways. Proverbs 16:31, "Gray hair is a crown of glory; it is attained along the path of righteousness." Along with this are words in Proverbs 20:29, "The glory of young men is their strength, and gray hair is the splendor of the old." In the detailed instruction being given to the people of God, Leviticus 19:32 (NASB) states: "You shall rise up before the gray-headed and honor the aged, and you shall revere your God; I am the Lord." The Pulpit Commentary states:

> *Reverence for the old is inculcated as being a part, not merely of natural respect, but of the fear of God. In the East this virtue, implying deference on the part of the strong to the weak, and of the inexperienced to the wise, exists in larger influence for good than in the West, where, however, its place has been, but only par-*

tially, supplied by the greater deference paid by man to woman.

Too often rather than the show of respect and honor toward the aged or gray-haired person or parent, there is deference (submission or compliance to/with the will or wishes of another) and/or condescension (patronizing, or voluntary assumption of equality with a person regarded as inferior) substituted. Deference and condescension are both insincere and are indicative of an inward reluctance to accept another person honorably or respectfully. One cannot, and should not ignore the simply stated words of Leviticus 19:32. The aged are to be respected and honored. It should be noted that respect and honor should be given because of one's fear of God the Lord.

Some introspection is appropriate at this point. Is respect and honor shown in a Biblical way toward the elderly in your sphere of relationships as well as within the Church you attend? For those who serve the Church in a professional way, is there respect and honor shown toward the aging members of the Church Courts (Presbytery, General Assembly, Church Councils)? The Head of the Church expects a showing respect and honor to all rather than to a select few. Some of the aged ones have come to accept the fact that equality, respect and honor is reserved for a few but not all. They begin to absent themselves more and more from the convocations rather than to attend and endure the indignity and tokenism of fake honor…or deference…or respect.

Some time ago, a friend who posts helpful and succinct words of encouragement on Facebook wrote about the act of "condescending". When used as a verb, it means: "to put aside one's assumed dignity, superiority or sense of importance voluntarily and assume equality with one who is regarded as being inferior." Is it a Biblical posture, attitude and behavior that is genuinely and consistently done? No! Is there a word that Jesus would use to describe this posture, attitude and behavior when it is insincerely done or ignored altogether? Yes! He would label it hypocrisy. It is an area where change and conformity to Scripture should occur and be the norm rather than the exception.

First Peter 2:16-18 sets a standard for one's posture, attitude and behavior for all kinds of circumstances and conditions. He wrote:
> *Treat everyone with high regard: Love the brotherhood of believers, fear God, honor the king. Servants, submit yourselves to your masters with all respect, not only to those who are good and gentle, but even to those who are unreasonable.*

Sadly, those who claim to be strict followers of Jesus Christ do not always treat everyone with high regard nor do they love the brotherhood as they should. Rather than positive words of respect and honor that can encourage and build another up, there are words of criticism. Rather than acceptance of another (Romans 15:7) there is an attitude and body language that models dismissiveness. Rather than treating others better than oneself (Philippians 2:4), they are treated as inferior or of little consequence.

For those who have taken time to view funeral services conducted on television, or attended a local funeral for an acquaintance, eulogies are almost always expected and have become a part of the service. One result is that sometimes a person becomes larger in death than they were in life. To say glowing comments makes attenders feel better about the sad occasion. If one attends enough funerals, one will probably leave with a thought – "I didn't know that about so and so." My own personal thought and hope is, if there are nice things one wishes to say about the deceased at a funeral, why not say it to the person beforehand rather than after their earthly departure? Why isn't kindness, respect and honor granted in one's lifetime rather than in death?

Some people, deservedly, may even have regrets because of their past relationship with the deceased. If they don't, they really should. Some people deserved honor and respect rather than animosity or retaliation. The disrespectful should use the funeral as a time for admitting their guilt and sin; confessing it to the Lord, and seeking His forgiveness for their personal ill-feelings and mistreatment of a brother or sister in Christ. It's never too late to get one's life and past actions right with the Lord. If you fail to adhere to God's Word now, there is a time coming when you'll wish that you had.

It would behoove the body of Christ to subscribe to the teaching of the Head of the Church – Jesus Christ. The words written by Charles H. Gabriel express a ministry the Church can and should maintain:

How good and pleasant is the sight
When brethren make it their delight
To dwell in blest accord;
Such love is like anointing oil
That consecrates for holy toil
The servants of the Lord.

...The Lord commands His blessing there,
And they that walk in love shall share
In life that never ends.

25. Perilous Times

But know this, that in the last day perilous times will come: For men will be lovers of themselves, lovers of money, boasters, proud, blasphemers, disobedient to parents, unthankful, unholy, unloving, unforgiving, slanderers, without self-control, brutal, despisers of good, traitors, headstrong, haughty (proud), lovers of pleasure rather than lovers of God, having a form of godliness but denying its power.
Second Timothy 3:3-5 (NKJV)

    Cultural decadence is rampant throughout the world. There is dysfunction within governments and families, as well as religious groups and a disinterested society. In many places, genocide occurs with little notice, reaction or response. Abortions continue as a means of population control. Foundational principles that were once cherished as a necessary part of life have eroded dramatically. There is the growing issue of unscreened illegal immigration and the inherent and potential terrorist dangers lurking therein. The moral values of the United States, as well as elsewhere in the world, tolerates and condones many things that God condemns. Some of these are indicated in Romans 1:18-31 and Second Timothy 3:3-5. Some of the eroding values include preservation of life; abstinence from substance abuse; a shift towards socialism as a lifestyle and for more progressive tolerance and governance.
    The apostle Paul was cognizant of the times in which he lived and the capacity of opponents of Christianity to ratchet up their hostilities to the Lord Jesus Christ and those who would serve Him. Paul would expound on and mention the vulnerability that one must be aware of if the desire is to serve the Lord faithfully and wholeheartedly. He wrote

(Second Corinthians 3:5): "Not that we are adequate in ourselves to consider anything as coming from ourselves, but our adequacy is from God." In oneself, there is an awareness of weakness and inability to accomplish the great task of reaching a generation with the message of the Gospel. Why is it so challenging to make God's Gospel known? When Paul wrote to Timothy, he wanted him to be aware of the environment in which he would be ministering. He wrote (First Timothy 4:1-2, NKJV), "The Spirit expressly says that in latter times some will depart from the faith, giving heed to deceiving spirits and doctrines of demons, speaking lies in hypocrisy, having their own conscience seared with a hot iron." He is indicating it will be difficult to find people committed to Jesus Christ alone and to establish camaraderie among those with fidelity to God's truth.

In his writing on Servanthood, Charles R. Swindoll shared his thoughts based upon Second Corinthians 10:8-12: "[We are] always carrying about in the body the dying of Jesus, so that the life of Jesus also may be manifested in our body. For we who live are constantly being delivered over to death for Jesus' sake..." He then wrote:

> *People who serve God and others carry about in the body signs of death—dangers and perils that are undeniable. Subtle and silent, these dangers lurk in the most unexpected places, pleading for satisfaction. The true servant is vulnerable. Servants of God are every bit as human and subject to the perils of life as any other person.*

How then should the servant of the Lord live and serve? What will be the result in one's becoming effective and impacting his/her generation for Jesus Christ? Can perilous times allow for Gospel outreach that will gain response regardless of the lurking dangers and impending peril? What was Paul anticipating as the message of Jesus Christ being the

Becoming A Servant

Savior was continually and constantly shared? The words he wrote in Philippians 1:20-21 are relevant for all of God's people in all ages.

> *I eagerly expect and hope that I will in no way be ashamed, but will have complete boldness, so that now as always Christ will be exalted in my body, whether by life or by death. For to me, to live is Christ, and to die is gain.*

Paul was always cognizant of the dangers, perils and consequences of representing Jesus Christ in a world that has chosen to detach itself from Christ and His kingdom. In Second Corinthians 11:23-28 (NKJV), Paul shares a litany of the things he endured to make Christ known. He begins with a question and then shares some of that which confronted him as a servant of Jesus Christ:

> *Are they ministers of Christ? (I speak as a fool) I am more — in labors more abundant, in stripes beyond measure, in prisons more frequent, in deaths often. From the Jews five times I received forty stripes less one. Thrice was I beaten with rods, once was I stoned; thrice I suffered shipwreck, a night and a day adrift in the deep; in journeyings often, in perils from waters, in perils from robbers, in perils from mine own countrymen, in perils from the heathen, in perils in the city, in perils in the wilderness, in perils in the sea, in perils among false brethren; in weariness and painfulness, in sleeplessness often, in hunger and thirst, in fasting often, in cold and nakedness. Besides those things which are external, there is that which cometh upon me daily: the care for all the churches!*

How many professing Christians do you know who would be willing to endure just one of the many things that Paul encountered? Most fail to participate due to very minor and relatively unimportant things. The focus and priority to live for Christ has been too often marginalized and reinterpreted as something much less than taking up one's cross daily and following in the footsteps of Jesus Christ. Charles R. Swindoll in *Insights for Living* wrote a devotional about servanthood. In it he said: "Jesus didn't go for the hype of influential celebrity types. He was a servant, not a superstar." His conclusion sounds very contrary to the celebrity church of the twenty-first century. Servanthood is best understood when one arrives at a point of knowing it is not just what one thinks or says that makes one a valid servant but also what one is becoming and doing. Becoming and doing the work of a servant flows out of conviction and commitment of what one must be and do in Jesus' name. Jesus, our Master, said (Matthew 10:16): "I am sending you (my servants) out like sheep among wolves. Therefore be as shrewd as snakes and as innocent as doves."

From an earth-side point of view, there may be some advantages to a political approach to life. Our world is all about who you know and "what have you done for me lately?" We are primed early on to look out for ourselves and to do whatever it takes to not miss the big break. But if one sees oneself as a follower of Christ, that kind of thinking bears little resemblance to His life and teaching. Take for instance the encounter that Jesus had with two of His most committed disciples. An encounter that only goes to prove that even the best of us can still have those political instincts alive and well, down-deep inside. The role of the one sent out by Jesus is stipulated in John 10:16, "I tell you, no servant is greater than his master, nor is a messenger greater than the one who sent him." A similar statement is made by Jesus in John 15:20-21,

> *Remember what I told you: A servant is not greater than his master. If they persecuted me, they will persecute you also. If they obeyed my teaching, they will*

Becoming A Servant

obey yours also. They will treat you this way because of my name, for they do not know the one who sent me.

One's mission for the Master will face many challenges and much opposition. Even from among those who should be identified with Jesus, there will be the aura of forsaking Him and repudiating His Word. The servant of the Lord follows a higher calling rather than seeking accommodation to secular conveniences. There is a goal, prize and commendation awaiting those who reliably serve the Lord despite the challenges and opposition. Matthew 25:23 states the commendation of the master, when he tells those to whom he has assigned specific responsibilities: "Well done, good and faithful servant! You have been faithful with a few things; I will put you in charge of many things. Enter into the joy of your master!"

O serve the Lord with gladness,
And come before His throne;
He is the great Creator,
And He is God alone;
The heavens declare His glory,
The earth His power displays;
While millions without number
To Him glad anthems raise.
Refrain:
O serve the Lord with gladness,
And come before His throne;
He is our great Redeemer,
And He is God alone.

~ Fanny Crosby (1894) ~

26. Salt and Light

You are the salt of the earth, but if the salt becomes tasteless, with what will it be salted. For nothing is it potent any longer except, having been cast out, to be trampled upon by men. You are the light of the world. A city lying on a hill is unable to be hidden. Nor do they light a lamp and put it under a basket, but upon the lampstand, and it gives light to all those in the house. Thus let your light shine before men, so that they may see your good works and they should glorify your Father in the heavens.
Matthew 5:13-16

Salt is good, but if the salt loses its savor, with what will it be seasoned? It is fit neither for the soil nor for the manure pile, and it is thrown out. He who has ears to hear, let him hear.
Luke 14:34

To be useful as a servant of the Lord, the reality of one being yielded to the Master is essential. The previous chapter stated that servanthood is not just what one thinks or says but what one is becoming and doing in obedience to the Master. One hindrance that some experience is the fear of how others will respond to the servant. On one occasion while the church where I was Pastor was working through the instructional book, *Evangelism Explosion* (written by: D. James Kennedy), I was out with two key men doing random evangelism canvassing ministry. It was a training session. As the team leader, I would take the first visit and demonstrate how the evangelism canvassing should be done. When it came to the turn of one of the men, he said to me: "Pastor, I'm scared doing this." Anyone doing canvassing ministry has an inner fear of the kind of reception one might receive. There is no way to know what is going on inside a home or apartment behind closed doors. What made this man's response significant is that he was a courageous man who had served for several years in law enforcement. He had experienced all kinds of reactions over the years while performing his duty. Jesus' desire for one to be both light and salt never came with an assurance that one would be positively received. As a matter of fact, He would indicate to His disciples (Luke 10:16) that there would be varying responses and results: "Whoever listens to you listens to Me; whoever rejects you rejects Me; and whoever rejects Me rejects the One who sent Me."

When dealing with being afraid and having a sense of fear, it is always appropriate to remember the words in Isaiah 40:10, "Do not fear, for I am with you; do not be afraid, for I am your God… I will surely help you…" In the devotional *Get More Strength For The Journey*, Thursday, August 10, 2018, Joseph Stowell wrote the encouraging words about one's propensity to be afraid:

I'll never forget hearing the Brooklyn Tabernacle Choir in concert. The sincerity and depth of feeling the singers brought to the music showed that it was more than a mere performance. When they sang I'm Not Afraid Anymore, you could tell that many of the singers identified with the experience of living in constant fear before they met Jesus—fear of violence, fear of not having enough money, fear of what might happen to their children, fear of not being able to get the drugs needed to feed their addictions, fear of every tomorrow.

Earlier, Charles R. Swindoll wrote in *Insight For Living*, August 6, 2018 additional encouraging words:
Since God has called us to be His salt-and-light servants in a bland, dark society, it will be necessary for us to commit ourselves to the task before us. Remember,

salt must not lose its taste, and light must not be hidden...I am responsible for my salt not losing its bite and my light not becoming obscure or hidden. Every once in a while it is helpful to ask some very hard questions of myself. True servants do more than talk. We refuse to become the rabbit-hole Christians John Stott speaks of, popping out of our holes and racing from our insulated caves to all-Christian gatherings only to rush back again. For salt to be tasted and for light to be seen, we must make contact. We are personally responsible.

Christian lives are marked by peaks and valleys. One can experience moments of great victories by faith but can become stalled and gripped by fear while sliding into the valley of defeat. It would be helpful for one to recall the keen insight into of David's confidence when he expressed the words of Psalm 23:4, "Even though I walk through the valley of the shadow of death, I will fear no evil, for You are with me..." The NLT expresses the key phrase: *"I will not be afraid, for you are close beside me."* This is the truth Jesus related to His disciples during their time of following Him. He reminds them that He is the Good Shepherd (John 10:14-15), "I am the good shepherd; I know my own sheep, and they know me, just as my Father knows me and I know the Father. So I sacrifice my life for the sheep."

A classic example of the peak and valley that can quickly become a reality in one's life is illustrated in First Kings 18-19. There has been an extended drought in the land that had been prophesied by Elijah. Elijah meets with Ahab and addresses the need to forsake Baalism and to turn to the Living God. To emphasize his point, Elijah proposes a contest between himself and the 450 prophets of Baal. The time, place and conditions are set. The prophets of Baal will beseech their God to send rain on the land. They persist for hours of imploring their god to respond. They intensify their sincerity by physical acts upon themselves. After hours of this futile exercise, Elijah will be front and center is his calling upon the true God Alone. A major issue with the people of that day is their inability and unwillingness to identify with the true God. First Kings 18:20-21 (NLT) describes the scene:

> *Ahab summoned all the people of Israel and the prophets to Mount Carmel. Then Elijah stood in front of them and said: How much longer will you waver, hobbling between two opinions? If the LORD is God, follow him! But if Baal is God, then follow him! But the people were completely silent.*

The words: "the people were completely silent" (or: they answered him not a word)" indicates the lack of commitment to anything religious or spiritual at all. Elijah would stand alone against the prophets of Baal. Elijah was unafraid even though he stood alone against the multitude. The text records the tremendous victory realized by the faith and action of the prophet of God. The Lord consumes the sacrifice offered by Elijah along with the altar. After this miraculous event, Elijah is confident that rain is imminent. He states to Ahab, First Kings 18:41, "…Go up, eat and drink, for there is the sound of a heavy rain."

Elijah goes up on Mount Carmel to watch and wait for the rain to begin. He sent his servant seven times to look toward the sea to determine if there was any indicator of God sending rain upon the land. What was Elijah seeking as a sign from God? What would it take for him to be convinced that God was about to act? On the seventh trip of the servant, he returns by saying (verse 44): "There is a cloud as small as a man's hand rising from the sea." That's all the indication Elijah needed. A cloud the size of a man's hand convinced Elijah that was God's sign that He was about to send rain upon the land. How much faith does it take for you to believe that

God is at work in your behalf and for the good of His people? Would you be convinced to believe by a cloud the size of a man's hand? What about if it was nothing more than a grain of mustard seed? Could you have faith at that level to believe great things from God? Verses 44-45 indicates: "Elijah replied: Go and tell Ahab, Prepare your chariot and go down before the rain stops you. Meanwhile, the sky grew dark with clouds and wind, and a heavy rain began to fall."

On Mount Carmel, Elijah was literally at a peak of victory and faith.

However, in First Kings 19, the scene will quickly change from a mountain peak of victory to a deep dark valley of despair. What brought about this dramatic change? It is caused by a death threat made in Verse 2, "Jezebel sent a messenger to Elijah, saying: May the gods deal with me, and ever so severely, if by this time tomorrow I do not make your life like the lives of those you killed!" Elijah should've known there was this lurking hostility and that which had been done to the prophets of Baal would not go unnoticed. When he Elijah heard Jezebel's words, he was seized with fear and became afraid for his life. Verses 3-4 are a sad commentary about the quick reversal by Elijah. As a man of great courage and boldness, he cringes and becomes afraid. The verses state:

> *Elijah was afraid and ran for his life. When he came to Beersheba in Judah, he left his servant there, while he himself traveled on a day's journey into the wilderness. He sat down under a broom tree and prayed that he might die. I have had enough, LORD, he said: Take my life, for I am no better than my fathers.*

His adrenalin must've been at a high level. He forgot about being salt and light as he traveled for a day to escape the reach and action of Jezebel. After a night, verse 8 indicates: "He walked forty days and forty nights until he reached Horeb, the mountain of God." It is conceivable that he not only was seeking escape from the reach of Jezebel, he was also seeking to escape the reach of God. Fear and being afraid can alter one's sound judgment. It can and does short-circuit faith and confidence in God. Fear can cloud the mind of a servant and child of God that can lead one into making incorrect decisions and choices. What will God do to and with His fearful and afraid prophet? Will He allow Him to just dangle in the lonely path he has chosen?

Verses 9-13 indicate the choice of Elijah, coming to a cave and lodging there, and the appearance and voice of God, "What are you doing here, Elijah?" God listens to the litany about his life and ministry and then states: "Go out and stand on the mount before the Lord." Elijah had asked for and experienced the powerful hand of God in the contest with the prophets of Baal. Now in a one on one encounter, he will experience the Lord passing by and a strong wind tearing the mountains apart and shattering the stones and rocks. The text indicates the Lord was not in that wind. After the wind, there was an earthquake that shook the ground, and then there was a fire but the Lord was not in either one. After the fire, there was the sound of a low and gentle whisper. With all of the thunderous and earthshaking experience, he will hear the whisper, the gentle and non-dramatic voice of God. Elijah must listen to that whisper. If/When he does, he will hear the specific question and instruction of God. The question, once again: "What are you doing here, Elijah?" The instruction from the Lord he must obey is (verse 15): "Go, return on your way to the wilderness of Damascus." He is also given specific undone work to go finish. He is to do that and complete his task. Elijah will learn that the Lord will deal with Jezebel who threatened death to Elijah, one of God's prophets. She will die a harsh death and her body will be devoured by dogs. The violent death she experiences is described in Second Kings 9:30-37.

Becoming A Servant

It would've been good if Elijah had known the principle taught by Jesus about being salt and light in the world. The role of a servant of the Lord is clearly and definitively stated in the Sermon on the Mount by Jesus Christ, Matthew 5:13-16,

> **You are the salt** *of the earth. But if the salt loses its savor, how can it be made salty again? It is no longer good for anything, except to be thrown out and trampled by men.* **You are the light** *of the world. A city on a hill cannot be hidden. Neither do people light a lamp and put it under a basket. Instead, they set it on a lampstand, and it gives light to everyone in the house. In the same way,* **let your light shine** *before men, that they may see your good deeds and glorify your Father in heaven.*

With reference to being light, a gospel song usually considered to be a children's Hymn expresses this truth from the Sermon on the Mount.

> *Jesus bids us shine with a pure, clear light,*
> *Like a little candle burning in the night.*
> *In this world of darkness so let us shine—*
> *You in your small corner, and I in mine.*
> *Jesus bids us shine, as we work for Him,*
> *Bringing those that wander from the paths of sin;*
> *He will ever help us, if we shine,*
> *You in your small corner, and I in mine.*
>
> ~ Susan B. Warner (1868) ~

27. Hearers Must Be Doers

Be ye doers of the word, and not hearers only, deceiving yourselves. For if anyone is a hearer of the word and not a doer, he is like a man observing his natural face in a mirror; for he observes himself, goes away, and immediately forgets what kind of man he was. But he who looks into the perfect law of liberty and continues in it, and is not a forgetful hearer but a doer of the work, this one will be blessed in what he does.
James 1:22-25 (NKJV)

  In a technological world where all kinds of information is available in written form and electronic devices, what does one really hear, know and do with the data received? Data is used as a basis for reasoning, discussion and calculation. In modern times, it assumes there will be dialogue with an individual or group rather than a monologue that would inform but be unable to discern whether or not there is any measurable interaction and applicable understanding.

  In the religious sector of the culture, there is a voluminous amount of information that is stated or written about all areas of church government and lifestyle choices. How much of Biblical instruction is incorporated into the twenty-first century Church? Is the example of Jesus Christ understood, desired and applied within the Church and by its members? For instance, Jesus prayed for the unity within His Church. Does unity exist and is it Biblically pursued by the Church and its members?

  If the above questions were answered affirmatively, it is curious about how many churches and denominations there are in the world. It is estimated there are 34,000 Christian denominations. Worldwide, the estimate for the number of church buildings is 37 million. Protestant Christianity makes up the bulk of different denominations – 9,000 main-stream and 22,000 independent (World Christian Encyclopedia). Many of the churches are stand-alone congregations, several of whom share essentially common beliefs but with little or no mutual association with one another.

These estimates are a sad commentary on how far churches have departed from the prayer of Jesus Christ, John 17:20-21,

My prayer is not for them alone. I pray also for those who will believe in me through their message, that all of them may be one, Father, just as you are in me and I am in you. May they also be in us so that the world may believe that you have sent me.

It also misses the point of Paul's admonition and prayer in Ephesians 4:3-6,

Make every effort to keep the unity of the Spirit through the bond of peace. There is one body and one Spirit, just as you were called to one hope when you were called; one Lord, one faith, one baptism; one God and Father of all, who is over all and through all and in all.

How seriously do we believe Jesus was when He prayed His prayer for unity? For whose benefit was His prayer offered? Did the religious movements of His day – scribes, Pharisees and Sadducees - eagerly receive and act upon the words in His prayer? Based upon the statistical analysis of the World Christian Encyclopedia, does the twenty-first century Christian community take the words of Jesus in His prayer seriously?

One of the great needs in the Church is for spiritual revival. The psalmist wrote and prayed in this regard, Psalm 85:4-7,

Becoming A Servant

Restore us, *O God of our salvation, and cause Your anger toward us to cease. Will You be angry with us forever? Will You prolong Your anger to all generations? Will You not **revive us** again, That Your people may rejoice in You?* ***Show us Your mercy****, Lord, and grant us **Your salvation**.*

Historically, there has always been a heart-cry for revival. One servant of the Lord who was direct in his thoughts about revival was Dr. A. W. Tozer. Some quotes attributed to him include:

Prayer is never an acceptable substitute for obedience. The sovereign Lord accepts no offering from His creatures that is not accompanied by obedience. To pray for revival while ignoring or actually flouting the plain precept laid down in the Scriptures is to waste a lot of words and get nothing for our trouble.

If the envious, the defamers and the backbiters were taken out of the average church, there would be revival overnight.

I believe that the imperative need of the day is not simply revival, but a radical reformation that will go to the root of our moral and spiritual maladies and deal with causes rather than with consequences, with the disease rather than with symptoms.

Our mistake is that we want God to send revival on our terms. We want to get the power of God into our hands, to call it to us that it may work for us in promoting and furthering our kind of Christianity. We want still to be in charge, guiding the chariot through the religious sky in the direction we want it to go, shouting Glory to God, but modestly accepting a share of the glory for ourselves in a nice inoffensive sort of way. We are calling on God to send fire on our altars; completely ignoring the fact that they are OUR altars and not God's.

Over the years, there were several men of God who addressed the need and desire for spiritual revival. Some of them shared the following thoughts:

Leonard Ravenhill:
I read of the revivals of the past, great sweeping revivals where thousands of men were swept into the Kingdom of God. I read about Charles G. Finney winning his thousands and his hundreds of thousands of souls to Christ. Then I picked up a book and read the messages of Charles G. Finney and the message of Jonathan Edwards on 'Sinners in the Hands of an Angry God,' and I said, 'No wonder men trembled; no wonder they fell in the altars and cried out in repentance and sobbed their way to the throne of grace!'

Oswald J. Smith:
In the Irish Revival of 1859, people became so weak that they could not get back to their homes. Men and women would fall by the wayside and would be found hours later pleading with God to save their souls. They felt that they were slipping into hell and that nothing else in life mattered but to get right with God... To them eternity meant everything. Nothing else was of any consequence. They felt that if God did not have mercy on them and save them, they were doomed for all time to come.

Becoming A Servant

Stephen Olford:
> *Whether it be in the personal life, or in the church life, or on the mission field, we need revival–we need revival urgently–we need revival desperately!*
>
> *Revival is the manifestation of the glory, power, and blessing of the Son of God among His people.*
>
> *Revival is ultimately Christ Himself, seen, felt, heard, living, active, moving in and through His body on earth.*
>
> *Revival is not some emotion or worked-up excitement; it is rather an invasion from heaven which brings to man a conscious awareness of God.*
>
> *Revival is that strange and sovereign work of God in which He visits His own people–restoring, reanimating, and releasing them into the fullness of His blessing.*
>
> *When God breaks into a life or a community, nothing else matters save the person of Jesus, the glory of Jesus, the name of Jesus. Perhaps the greatest barrier to revival on a large scale is the fact that we are too interested in a great display. We want an exhibition; God is looking for a man who will throw himself entirely on God. Whenever self-effort, self-glory, self-seeking or self-promotion enters into the work of revival, then God leaves us to ourselves.*
>
> *Will you pray 'Revive me!' and then open your being to the Spirit of Revival? Do not rest until you have been restored to the fullness of the blessing that God is waiting to pour out in your life!*

D. Martyn Lloyd-Jones:
> *Does it grieve you my friends, that the name of God is being taken in vain and desecrated? Does it grieve you that we are living in a godless age...But, we are living in such an age and the main reason we should be praying about revival is that we are anxious to see God's name vindicated and His glory manifested. We should be anxious to see something happening that will arrest the nations, all the peoples, and cause them to stop and to think again.*

C. H. Spurgeon's impassioned words:
> *Oh! men and brethren, what would this heart feel if I could but believe that there were some among you who would go home and pray for a revival men whose faith is large enough, and their love fiery enough to lead them from this moment to exercise unceasing intercessions that God would appear among us and do wondrous things here, as in the times of former generations.*

One of the more recent revival efforts emphasizes a needed paradigm that should be embraced, applied and activated within the Church. It is based upon the need for the believer(s) to remember, repent (change), return and recover.

In Revelation 2 and 3, Jesus is walking in the midst of the seven churches. He assesses Where they are in terms of His value for functional ministry. A phrase that is attached to His observation about the churches is in the form of a summary of His expectation for those who name His name, "Whoever has ears, let them hear what the Spirit says to the churches." The words of the Head of the Church address the danger of abandoning the first love one had for Christ and His Church (Revelation 2:4); allowing fear to replace faith when ties of suffering are closing in on one's life (Revelation 2:10);

Becoming A Servant

Carelessly allowing false teaching and doctrines to infiltrate (Revelation 2:14-15); the tolerance of immorality within the Church (Revelation 2:20-24); the reality and presence of complacency, lethargy and lifelessness (Revelation 3:1-2); laziness, incorrect assessment and indifference that has allowed for a group becoming lukewarm in terms of the truth of God and His mission for His people (Revelation 3:15-17).

Only one of the seven Churches is commended by Jesus Christ. His words of encouragement to the Church at Philadelphia is: "I know your deeds. I have placed before you an open door that no one can shut. I know that you have little strength, yet you have kept my word and have not denied my name" (Revelation 3:8). All of the churches hear His words: "Whoever has ears, let them hear what the Spirit says to the churches."

WHAT IF the churches of our day gave heed to the scrutiny and words of Jesus Christ, would it affect them in any way? Would they desire to "repent" and get on the pathway of Jesus Christ for His Church? Is the Church you attend the Church of the Lord Jesus Christ or controlled by strong natural leaders who are allowed to influence the direction, mission and ministry of the local Church? Should you attend and continue to support a Church that is dying and in a terminal state? Why, or why not?

The prayer of God's people should include and echo the words of the Psalmist who craved and cherished a closer relationship with the Lord.

Psalm 139:23-24

> *Search ME, O God, and know MY heart. Try ME, and know MY thoughts. And see if there be any grievous (wicked) way in ME, and lead ME in the everlasting way.*

Psalm 19:14

Let the words of MY mouth and the meditation of MY heart be acceptable in YOUR sight, O Lord, MY rock and MY redeemer.

Promise Keepers was funded in 1990 by Bill McCartney, then the Head Football Coach at the University of Colorado in Boulder, Colorado. He got the idea for Promise Keepers after attending a Fellowship of Christian Athletes banquet in Pueblo, Colorado where he had yielded his life to Jesus Christ. As Promise Keepers developed into a ministry, Bill McCartney developed a curriculum that emphasized *Personal Holiness In Times of Temptation.* One of the choruses written for this ministry – *Purify My Heart* - became the theme prayer. Some of the words are:

Purify MY heart,
Cleanse ME from within and
make ME holy.
Cleanse ME from my sin,
deep within.

Refiner's fire,
MY heart's one desire
Is to be... holy;
Set apart for You, Lord.

Are these words you are ready to pray? Is this a commitment you are ready to make? Is this a life you will purpose to live? Be a doer and not just a hearer of God's Word! The one who is a doer of God's Word will be blessed in what he does (James 1:25).

28. Learning to Pray

And when you pray, do not be like the hypocrites. For they love to pray standing in the synagogues and on the street corners to be seen by men...when you pray, go into your inner room, shut your door, and pray to your Father, who is unseen. And your Father, who sees what is done in secret, will reward you. And when you pray, do not babble on like pagans, for they think that by their many words they will be heard. Do not be like them, for your Father knows what you need before you ask Him.
Matthew 6:5-8

One of the lessons to learn about prayer is to keep in mind that prayer is being offered before our Father, who dwells in heaven. He knows what you need before you ask Him. Romans 8:26-27 reminds us that:

> *The Spirit helps us in our weakness. For we do not know how we ought to pray, but the Spirit Himself intercedes for us with groans too deep for words. And He who searches our hearts knows the mind of the Spirit, because the Spirit intercedes for the saints according to the will of God.*

To know that one's humble efforts of bringing requests before the Heavenly Father are aided by the ministry of the Holy Spirit who conforms the requests with the will of God, is both amazing and encouraging. It should fill one with faith, hope and confidence to know that the God of heaven is interested in the one who seeks His aide for one's earthly needs and struggles. I frequently remember and review the words of a prayer hymn, sometimes humming the melody, as I reflect before the Heavenly Father in prayer. The words were written by Albert S. Reitz,

> *Teach me to pray, Lord, teach me to pray;*
> *This is my heart-cry day unto day;*
> *I long to know Thy will and Thy way;*
> *Teach me to pray, Lord, teach me to pray.*

Chorus:
> *...Grant me Thy power, boundless and free,*
> *Power with men and power with Thee.*

These words are meaningful and purposeful as one approaches the throne of grace and mercy. They reflect a longing that was in the hearts of the disciples of Jesus who desired to know how they should pray to access the power that is boundless and free. They wanted to be able to do among the people that which Jesus Christ was doing both in word and in deed. Ultimately they would have to learn the distinction between knowing and doing the requirements to "pray without ceasing."

A perspective regarding persistence in prayer was shared in a devotional written by C. H. Spurgeon:

> *God's seasons are not at your beck. If the first stroke of the flint doth not bring forth the fire, you must strike again. God will hear prayer, but He may not answer it at the time which we in our minds have appointed; He will reveal Himself to our seeking hearts, but not just when and where we have settled in our own expectations. Hence the need of perseverance and importunity in supplication... Never let us despair. God's time for mercy will come; yea, it has come, if our time for believing has arrived. Ask in faith nothing wavering; but never cease from petitioning because the King delays to reply. Strike the steel again. Make the sparks fly and have your tinder ready; you will get a light before long.*

Becoming A Servant

Inasmuch as people would often refer to Jesus as the Rabbi (teacher, master), the disciples would've been seen as a type of rabbinical follower and student. Their job was to follow and to learn. After learning, acting upon that which was learned was required. In modern times, Rabbinical Schools are still functioning and young men (in some instances women also) are enrolled and learning the rituals, liturgies and customs that are to be observed and performed by the Rabbi. The Rabbinical School has sessions to teach those seeking to become Rabbis how to pray. It is stated in their enrollment catalogue:

We begin each morning with spirited communal tefila (prayer) in the beit midrash (a Jewish study hall located in a synagogue or other building). In this tranquil space, we have created a dynamic and meaningful prayer community in which we welcome and encourage engagement with traditional Jewish liturgy and prayer forms as well as experimentation and creativity. Some...prayer services involve a full, traditional liturgy. Other mornings, it is a more contemplative experience with meditation and chanting. Students are expected to attend morning tefila at least two days a week.

The modern Rabbinical School doubtlessly models itself after the traditions passed down from early days of Jewish religious practices. How effective are the traditional liturgies, prayer forms and rituals? Is this the type of prayer that Jesus addressed as He taught His disciples? Is Matthew 6:7 (NLT) relevant with some religious church customs, traditions and rituals? Jesus said: "When you pray, don't babble on and on as people of other religions do. They think their prayers are answered merely by repeating their words again and again." On a personal basis, as or when you pray, does the Heavenly Father construe your words to be "babble" or a heart-cry for

His intercession and intervening in your behalf? Does He respond according to your wants or to His defined needs of one's life? Someone wisely stated: "The Lord responds to one's need, not to one's greed." Rabbi Benjamin Blech wrote in his book, *Taking Stock: A Spiritual Guide To Rising Above Life's Ups and Downs:*
> *Greed will always leave you dissatisfied because you will never be able to get everything you desire. Greed never allows you to think you have enough; it always destroys you by making you strive ever harder for more.*

In The Parable of the Rich Fool, Luke 12:13-21, Jesus said: "Watch out! Guard yourselves against every form of greed, for a man's life does not consist in the abundance of his possessions." The focus of the parable is about a rich man who built more and more buildings in which he could store all of what he thought he needed for a long future. Part of the warning of Jesus to His followers is summarized in verses 20-21,
> *But God said to him, You fool! This very night your life will be required of you. Then who will own what you have accumulated? This is how it will be for anyone who stores up treasure for himself but is not rich toward God.*

There is (2018) an interesting evening program on Fox Business Network called, *"Strange Inheritances."* After reviewing the treasures that have been saved and passed down to other generations, every program closes with the hostess stating: "Remember! You can't take it with you!"

The Word of God is very clear about a person who has a desire to accumulate money and things. Ecclesiastes 5:10, "Whoever loves money never has enough; whoever loves wealth is never satisfied with their income. This too is meaningless." Similarly, the words of Hebrews 13:5 states, "Keep your lives free from the love of money and be content with what you have, because God has said: Never will I leave you; never will I forsake you."

Peter shared with those who would assume greater responsibilities with the people of God, First Peter 5:1-3,

> *To the elders among you…Be shepherds of God's flock that is under your care, watching over them—not because you must, but because you are willing, as God wants you to be; not pursuing dishonest gain, but eager to serve; not lording it over those entrusted to you, but being examples to the flock.*

The words "not pursuing dishonest gain" should not go unnoticed or unheeded. Part of the overall life of a disciple and follower of Jesus Christ is for one to be an example of Biblical values, standards and lifestyle.

An outworking of learning to pray must be seen in one's walking by faith alone in Christ alone. Imbedded in one's spiritual being should be the words from the Sermon on the Mount, Matthew 6:19-21,

> *Do not store up for yourselves treasures on earth, where moth and rust destroy, and where thieves break in and steal. But store up for yourselves treasures in heaven, where moth and rust do not destroy, and where thieves do not break in and steal. For where your treasure is, there your heart will be also.*

How did Jesus want His disciples to implement this principle within their prayer life? He almost immediately reminded them, Matthew 6:25, 31-33 -

> *Do not worry about your life, what you will eat or drink; or about your body, what you will wear. Is not life more than food, and the body more than clothes? Do not worry, saying, What shall we eat? or What*

shall we drink? or What shall we wear? For the pagans pursue all these things, and your Heavenly Father knows that you need them. But seek first the kingdom of God and His righteousness, and all these things will be added unto you.

The sooner these words of Jesus are heard, learned, known and applied, the sooner the greed issue will become a moot point and the faith principle grasped. Will it be an easy teaching and principle to be acted upon? Probably not! As this principle is integrated into one's life, it will be seen in one's acts of mercy and compassion; in ministering to the widows and orphans with compassion and kindness; by sharing with others that which is essential for their basic needs in life.

This faith principle in action was reflected in the life of a dear servant of the Lord, Stella B., who kept herself abreast of the needs of many people throughout the community where she lived. She was known to walk up to a person and ask what size shoes they wore. After hearing the size, she asked if they had another pair of shoes at home. She would then stake her claim on that extra pair of shoes because she knew someone who did not have any shoes to wear. There was an occasion when my mother-in-law was made aware that a poor family with two daughters had special needs. The girls had only one dress between them. As a result, they would alternate days when they could go to school. As soon as my mother-in-law learned about this situation, she called friends and neighbors with daughters of the same age and asked for extra clothes for these children. They responded and the girls were able to go to school together rather than on alternate days.

Learning to pray requires one to gain a heart of compassion, mercy and benevolence. It also entails action on the part of the one praying in faith. It is learning a lesson that James addressed (James 2:14-17) when he wrote about the correlation of faith and works. His words are clear:

Becoming A Servant

What good is it...if someone claims to have faith, but has no deeds? Can such faith save him? Suppose a brother or sister is without clothes and daily food. If one of you tells him, Go in peace; stay warm and well fed, but does not provide for his physical needs, what good is that? So too, faith by itself, if it is not complemented by action, is dead.

The word "faith" could also encompass and attach itself to "prayer." Learning to pray, and actually praying Biblically, cannot be done in a vacuum and be devoid of action. The words of commitment that can be our prayer of action were written by Frances R. Havergal (1874),

Take my life and let it be
Consecrated, Lord, to Thee.

Take my moments and my days,
Let them flow in endless praise.

Take my hands and let them move
At the impulse of Thy love.

Take my feet and let them be
Swift and beautiful for Thee.

Prayer should be more than a religious ritualistic approach where the same words are repeated over and over again. Prayer needs to be understood as an offering up of our desires unto God, for things agreeable to His will, in the name of Christ, with confession of our sins, and thankful acknowledgment of His mercies. Some of the important factors one should remember and be committed to include first and foremost Trust (Faith) in the Lord at all times (Psalm 62:8); Coming before Him humbly with a prepared heart that will cause God's ear to hear (Psalm 10:17); Approaching the throne of grace and mercy with confidence that He hears us and will disclose more of His will for one's life (I John 5:14); Believing the promise of Jesus Christ that whatever we ask the Father in Jesus' name will be met with favorable response (John 16:23); Approaching the Lord with one's requests about everything in prayer and supplication – along with thanksgiving – and making them known to God (Philippians 4:6).

The words written by William Bradbury (1861) should result in one's comfort, hope, peace and increasing confidence:

Sweet hour of prayer! sweet hour of prayer!
That calls me from a world of care,
And bids me at my Father's throne
Make all my wants and wishes known…

Sweet hour of prayer! sweet hour of prayer!
Thy wings shall my petition bear
To Him whose truth and faithfulness
Engage the waiting soul to bless.
And since He bids me seek His face,
Believe His Word and trust His grace,
I'll cast on Him my every care,
And wait for thee, sweet hour of prayer!

Epilogue

Servanthood is not based upon what one thinks, or even that which one says. Servanthood is always based upon that which one does and continues doing. To serve the Lord is a privilege. He has entrusted to His own the responsibility to represent Him well in the world. There are words that serve as an encouragement for the child of God. Some of those words are:

Dr. A. W. Tozer wrote:
> *The ideal Christian is one who knows he is free to do as he will and wills to be a servant. This is the path Christ took; blessed is the man who follows Him.*

John 12:26 - the words of Jesus Christ:
> *Whoever serves me must follow me; and where I am, my servant also will be. My Father will honor the one who serves me.*

William Gaither wrote the lyrics and music to:
> *I will serve Thee because I love Thee You have given life to me...*

Psalm 100 - is a challenge for all people in all ages:
> *Serve the Lord with gladness....*

Matthew 25:23 and Revelation 22:3
> *Well done, good and faithful servant.*

We must make as the prayer of our lives the words of a chorus:

James Perry

Make me a servant, Humble and meek;
Lord let me lift up Those who are weak;
And may the prayer Of my heart always be…
Make me a servant today!

You have the option of obeying the Lord's directives or choosing a pathway of your own design. The most logical and obvious choice would be to serve the Master - Jesus Christ - faithfully and well. You'll never regret centering your life in the will and plan of God for it.

About the Author

James Perry has served the Church with more than 54 years of continuous ministry. He attended Columbia Bible College (now Columbia International University) for three years; transferring to Covenant College, a new Presbyterian College in St. Louis, MO from which he graduated with a B.A. in Philosophy. After graduation, he enrolled in Covenant Theological Seminary where he received a B.D. in theology, and returned later for his M.A. He and his wife make their home in Centreville, AL; He has four children; 16 Grandchildren and 14 Great Grandchildren. He is the Author of 11 Books (all of which are available on Amazon).

www.ingramcontent.com/pod-product-compliance
Lightning Source LLC
Chambersburg PA
CBHW060823050426
42453CB00008B/566